Show me

MS-DOS 6

A Visual Guide to the Basics

Faithe Wempen

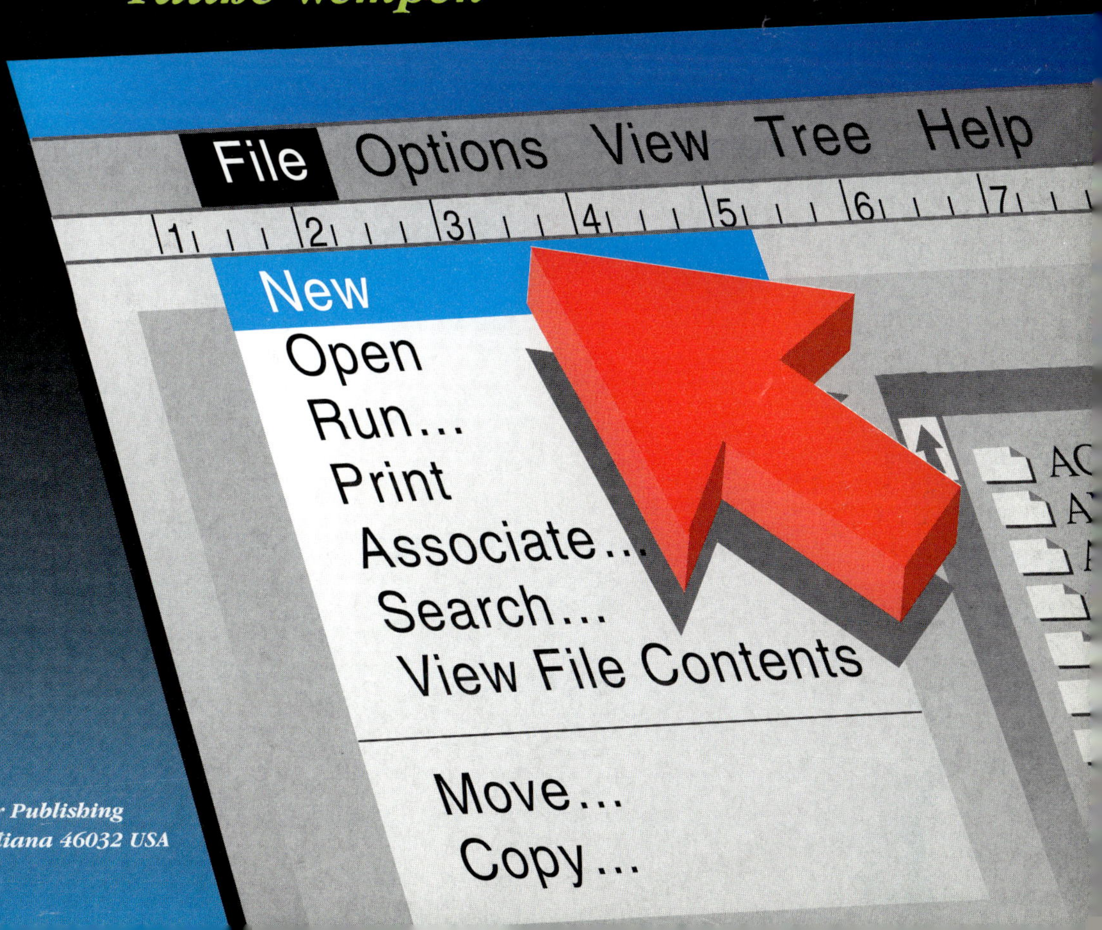

alpha books

A Division of Prentice Hall Computer Publishing

11711 North College Avenue, Carmel, Indiana 46032 USA

International Standard Book Number: 1-56761-237-7
Library of Congress Catalog Card Number: 93-71226

95 94 93 8 7 6 5 4 3 2 1

Interpretation of the printing code: the rightmost number of the first series of numbers is the year of the book's printing; the rightmost number of the second series of numbers is the number of the book's printing. For example, a printing code of 93-1 shows that the first printing of the book occurred in 1993.

Screen reproductions in this book were created by means of the program Collage Plus from Inner Media, Inc., Hollis, NH.

Printed in the United States of America

TRADEMARKS

All terms mentioned in this book that are known to be trademarks have been appropriately capitalized. Alpha Books cannot attest to the accuracy of this information. Use of a term in this book should not be regarded as affecting the validity of any trademark or service mark.

Publisher

Marie Butler-Knight

Associate Publisher

Lisa A. Bucki

Managing Editor

Elizabeth Keaffaber

Acquisitions Manager

Stephen R. Poland

Development Editor

Seta Frantz

Manuscript Editor

San Dee Phillips

Cover Designer

Scott Fullmer

Designer

Amy Peppler-Adams

Indexer

Jeanne Clark

Production Team

Diana Bigham, Katy Bodenmiller, Jodie Cantwell, Scott Cook, Tim Cox, Mark Enochs, Linda Koopman, Tom Loveman, Roger Morgan, Joe Ramon, Carrie Roth, Greg Simsic

Special thanks to C. Herbert Feltner for ensuring the technical accuracy of this book.

CONTENTS

INTRODUCTION

Have you ever said to yourself, "I wish someone would just *show me* how to use DOS." If you have, this *Show Me* book is for you. In it, you won't find detailed explanations of what's going on in your computer each time you enter a command. Instead, you will see pictures that *show you*, step by step, how to perform a particular task.

This book will make you feel as though you have your very own personal trainer standing next to you, pointing at the screen and showing you exactly what to do.

WHAT IS MS-DOS?

MS-DOS stands for Microsoft Disk Operating System. Microsoft periodically updates MS-DOS and issues new versions of it; this book is about MS-DOS 6.0. But let's skip the long formal name and just call the product "DOS."

DOS has two functions:

1. It's a coordinator, keeping all the computer parts working together (like the keyboard, monitor, and disk drive).

2. It's an interpreter, translating the commands you issue into machine language that the monitor, processor, disk drive, and so on can understand.

DOS is like the "conscious mind" of the computer. When DOS is running, the computer is "awake" and able to accept your instructions. Without DOS, your computer isn't useful for anything. Almost all computers start DOS automatically when you turn on the power.

TIP

If your computer does not start DOS automatically, DOS may not be installed. You may see a message such as **No System**. If so, turn to the Installation Guide in the back of this book to learn how to install DOS on your computer.

What Does DOS Look Like?

DOS has several appearances, or "faces." The most basic face is the command prompt, also called "DOS prompt." You'll learn how to issue commands from the command prompt in Part II of this book.

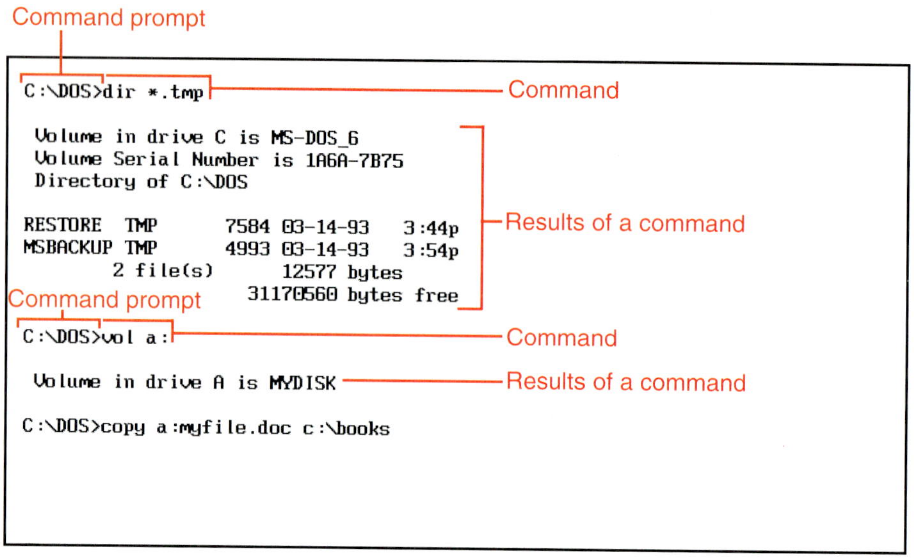

Beginners often prefer a friendlier face for DOS. The DOS Shell (sometimes called DOSSHELL) provides it. The DOS Shell is a program that comes with DOS. When you run it, you can enter DOS commands using graphical menus and boxes rather than by typing commands. You'll learn about the DOS Shell in Part I of this book.

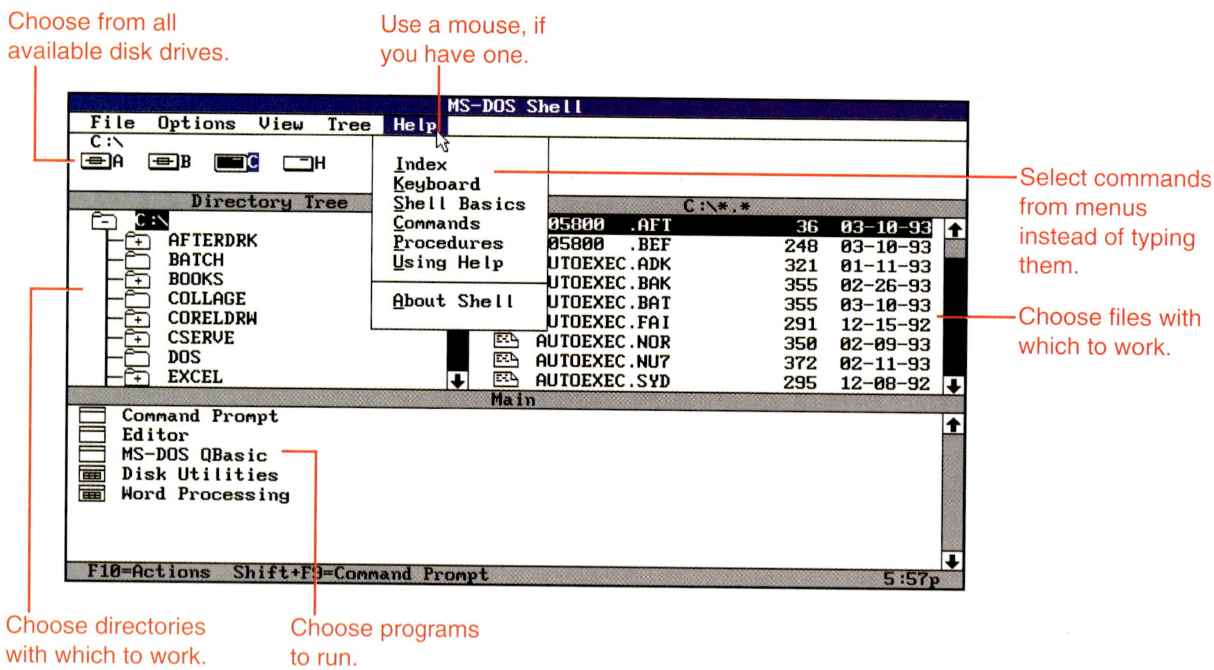

DOS 6 also comes with several utility programs that let you take control of your computer. Each utility program has its own face; you'll learn to use the most important ones in Part III of this book.

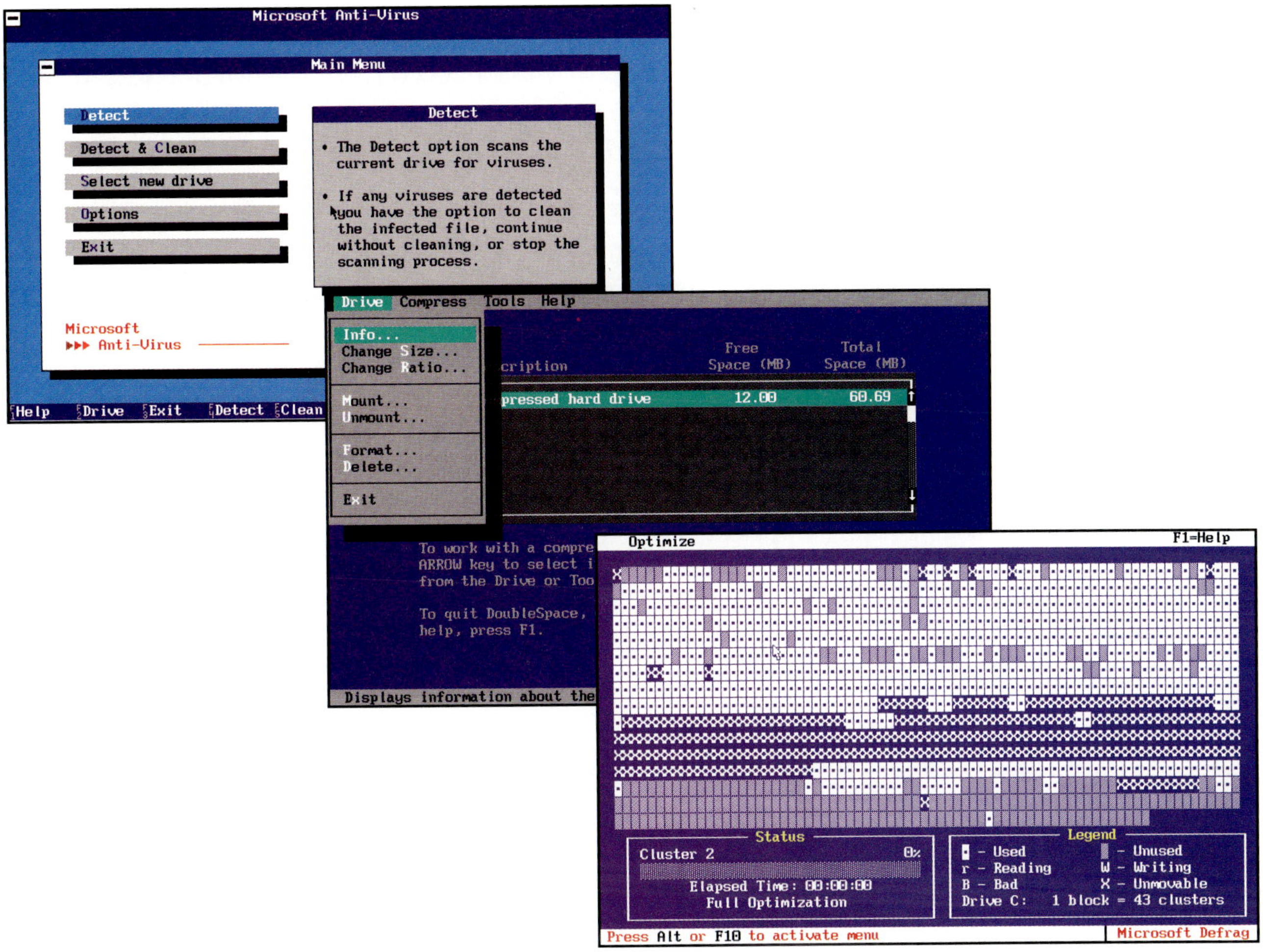

HOW TO USE THIS BOOK

Using this book is as simple as falling off your chair. Just flip to the task that you want to perform and follow the steps. You will see easy step-by-step instructions that tell you which keys to press and which commands to select. You will also see step-by-step pictures that show you what to do. Follow the steps or the pictures (or both) to complete the task. Here's an example of a set of instructions from this book.

Selecting a Single File

1. Click anywhere within the **File List**, or press **Tab** until the File List is active.

2. Click on the file, or press the up or down arrow keys to highlight the file.

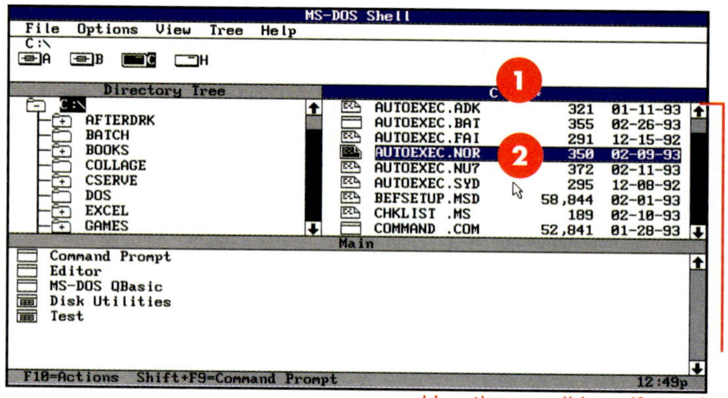

Use the scroll bar, if needed,

Every computer book has its own way of telling you which buttons to push and which keys to press. Here's how this book handles those formalities:

- Keys that you should press appear as they do on your keyboard (for example, press **Alt**, or press **F10**). If you need to press more than one key at once, the keys are separated with plus signs. For example, if the text tells you to press **Alt+F**, hold down the **Alt** key while pressing the **F** key.
- Text that you should type is printed in **boldface type like this**.
- Some features are activated by selecting a menu and then a command. If I tell you to "select **F**ile **C**opy," you should open the **F**ile menu and select the **C**opy command. In this book, the selection letter is printed in boldface for easy recognition.

Definitions in Plain English

In addition to the basic step-by-step approach, pages may contain Learn the Lingo definitions to help you understand key terms. These definitions are placed off to the side, so you can easily skip them.

> **LEARNING THE LINGO**
>
> **Pull-down menu:** A menu that appears at the top of the screen, listing various commands. The menu is not visible until you select it from the menu bar. The menu then drops down, covering a small part of the screen.

Quick Refreshers

If you need to know how to perform some other task in order to perform the current task, look for a Quick Refresher. With the Quick Refresher, you won't have to flip through the book to learn how to perform the other task; the information is right where you need it.

QUICK REFRESHER

Making dialog box selections

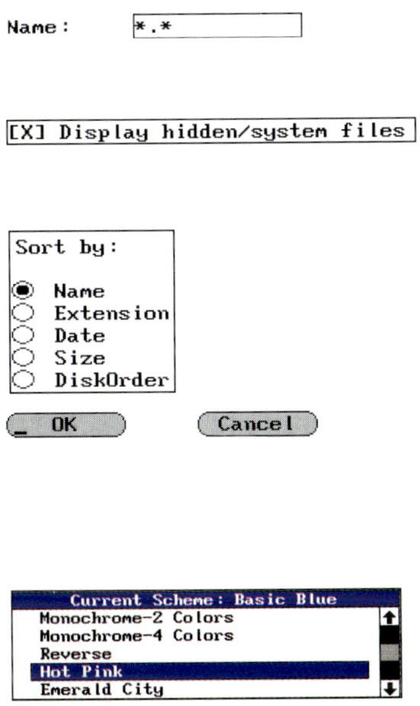

Text box. Click to place the I-beam in the box. Type your entry.

Check box. Click on a box to select or deselect it. (You can select more than one.)

Option button. Click on a button to select it. (You can select only one button in a group.)

Command button. Click on a button to execute the command. (All dialog boxes have at least two command buttons: OK to execute your selections, and Cancel to cancel the selections.)

List box. Click on a list item to choose it. Use the scroll bar to view additional items.

Tips, Ideas, and Shortcuts

Throughout this book, you will encounter tips that provide important information about a task or tell you how to perform the task more quickly. You will also come across some tips that tell you how to put the task to some practical use.

TIP

You can use Alt instead of F10; they both work the same. Alt is used in many programs as the key that activates the menu system, so learning to use Alt rather than F10 may prepare you better for learning other programs.

TIP

Here are some keyboard shortcuts for working with the DOS Shell:

Refresh Screen	F5
Move	F7
Copy	F8
Exit DOS Shell	ALT + F4

Exercises

Because most people learn by doing, several exercises throughout the book give you additional practice performing a task.

The DOS program files are kept in a special directory, usually called DOS, on drive C. Follow these steps to activate that directory.

1. If drive C is not the active drive, click on it, or press **Ctrl+C**.

2. Click on the **DOS** directory on the Directory Tree, or **Tab** until the Directory Tree area is active, and then use the arrow keys to highlight the **DOS** directory.

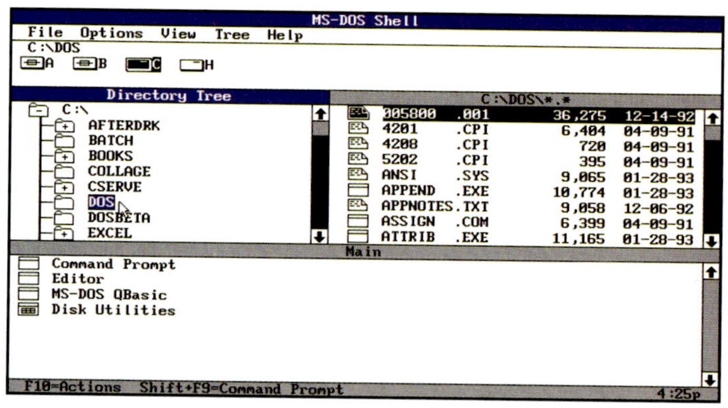

Now that the DOS directory is active, its files appear in the File List.

Where Should You Start?

If this is your first encounter with computers, read the next section, "Quick Computer Tour," before reading anything else. This section explains some computer basics that you need to know in order to get your computer up and running.

Once you know the basics, you can work through this book from beginning to end or skip around from task to task, as needed. If you decide to skip around, there are several ways you can find what you're looking for:

- Use the Table of Contents at the front of this book to find a specific task you want to perform.
- Use the complete index at the back of this book to look up a specific task or topic and find the page number on which it is covered.
- Use the color-coded sections to find groups of related tasks.
- Flip through the book, and look at the task titles at the top of the pages. This method works best if you know the general location of the task in the book.
- Use the inside back cover of this book to quickly find the page on which a command you are looking for is covered.

QUICK COMPUTER TOUR

If this is your first time in front of a computer, the next few sections will teach you the least you need to know to get started.

Parts of a Computer

Think of a computer as a car. The system unit holds the engine that powers the computer. The monitor is like the windshield that lets you see where you're going. And the keyboard and mouse are like the steering wheel, which allow you to control the computer.

The System Unit

The system unit contains three basic elements: a central processing unit (CPU), which does all the "thinking" for the computer; random-access memory (RAM), which stores instructions and data while the CPU is processing it; and disk drives, which store information permanently on disks to keep the information safe. It also contains several ports (at the back), which allow you to connect other devices to it, such as a keyboard, mouse, and printer.

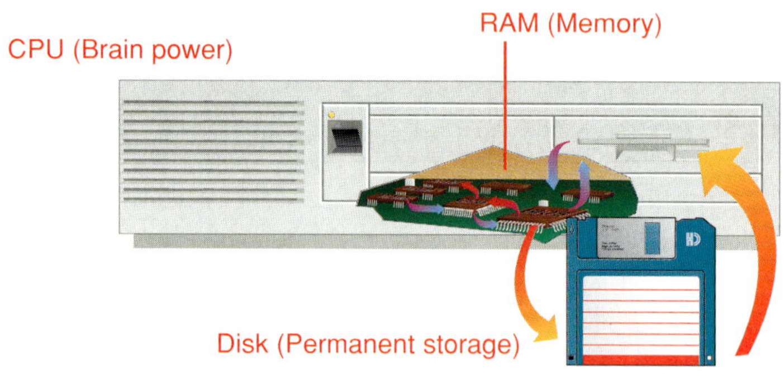

Using a Keyboard

The keyboard is no mystery. It contains a set of alphanumeric (letter and number) keys for entering text, arrow keys for moving around on-screen, and function keys (F1, F2, and so on) for entering commands. It also has some odd keys, including Alt (Alternative), Ctrl (Control), and Esc (Escape) that perform special actions.

Using a Mouse

Like the keyboard, a mouse allows you to communicate with the computer. You roll the mouse around on your desk to move a *mouse pointer* on-screen. You can use the pointer to open menus and select other items on-screen. Here are some mouse techniques you must master:

Pointing. To point, roll the mouse on your desk until the tip of the mouse pointer is on the item to which you want to point.

Clicking. To click on an item, point to the desired item, and then hold the mouse steady while you press and release the mouse button. Use the left mouse button unless I tell you specifically to use the right button.

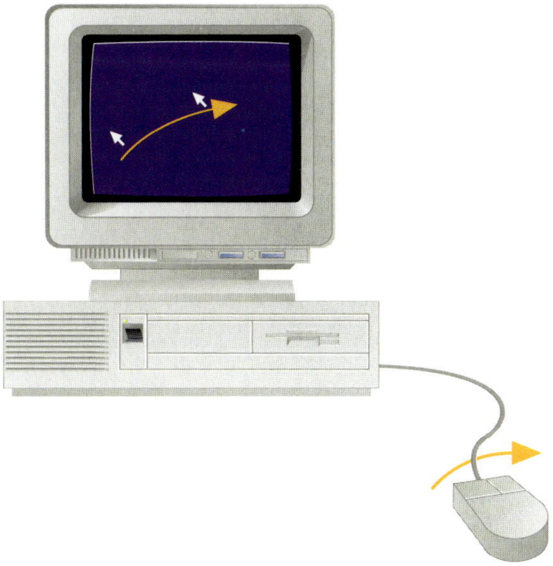

Double-clicking. To double-click, hold the mouse steady while you press and release the left mouse button twice quickly.

Right-clicking. To right-click, click using the right mouse button instead of the left button.

Understanding Disks, Directories, and Files

Whatever you type (a letter, a list of names, a tax return) is stored only in your computer's temporary memory and is erased when the electricity is turned off. To protect your work, you must save it in a *file* on a *disk*.

A *file* is like a folder that you might use to store a report or a letter. You name the file, so you can later find and retrieve the information it contains.

Save whatever you type in a named file.

Files are stored on *disks*. Your computer probably has a *hard disk* inside it (called drive C) to which you can save your files. You can also save files to *floppy disks*, which you insert into the slots (the floppy disk drives) on the front of the computer.

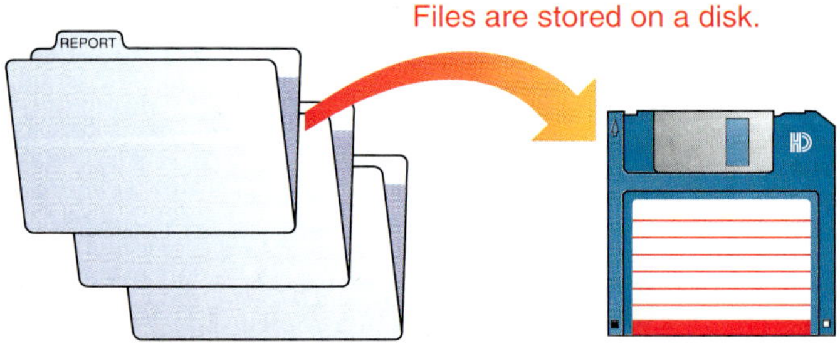

Files are stored on a disk.

To keep files organized on a disk, you can create *directories* on the disk. Each directory acts as a drawer in a filing cabinet, storing a group of related files. Although you can create directories on both floppy and hard disks, most people use directories only on hard disks.

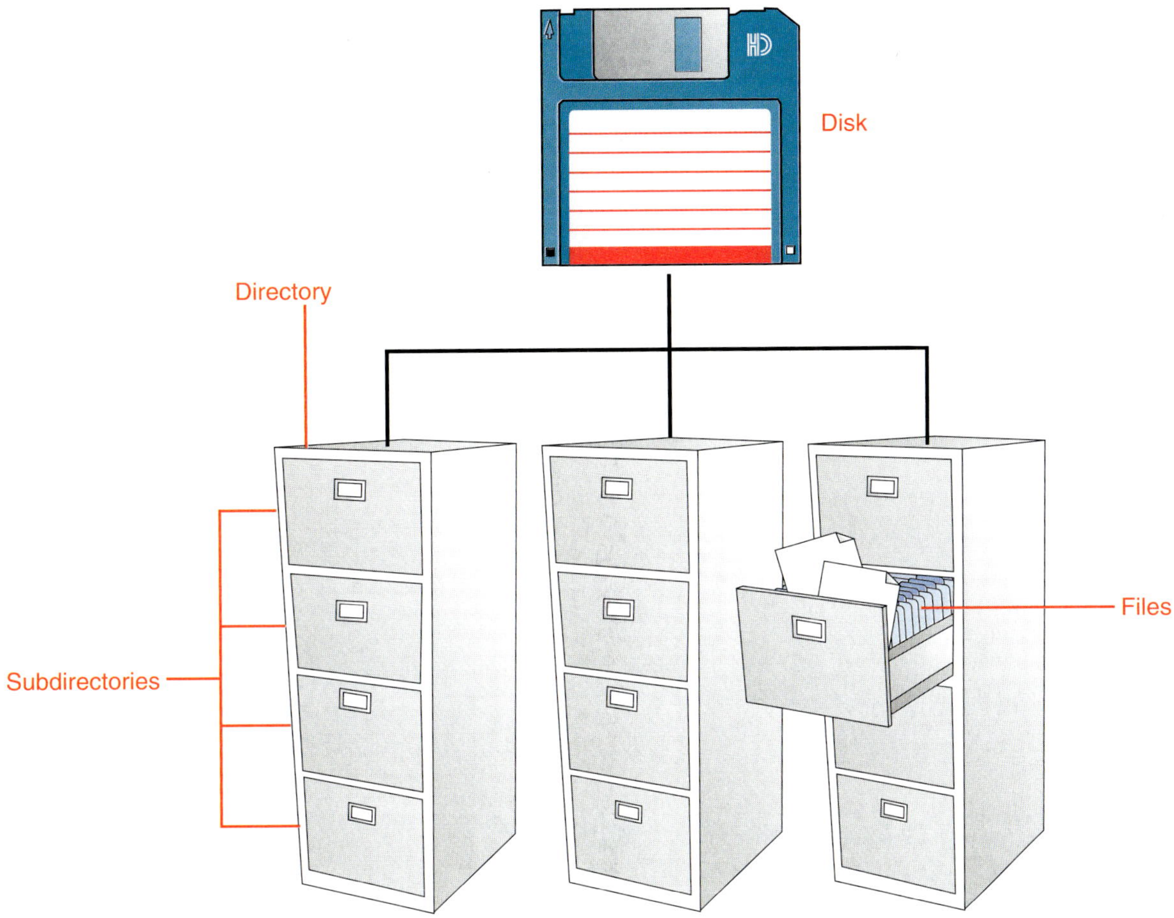

Now that you know a little something about your computer, it's time to dive into DOS. If you're a complete beginner, turn to Part I first and ease into DOS with the DOS Shell. If you have some experience, or are just feeling adventurous and intrepid, jump to Part II, where you'll learn to enter commands at the DOS prompt. If you're an experienced DOS user who just needs help with the new utilities provided in DOS 6, start with Part III, where you'll see some of the most useful new utilities in action.

PART 1

The DOS Shell

In this section, you'll learn to use the DOS Shell. The DOS Shell is a graphical environment that makes it easier for you to run DOS commands. Instead of typing commands at a boring prompt, you can choose from menus and use a mouse.

In this section, you'll learn:

- Starting the DOS Shell
- Navigating the DOS Shell screen
- Changing the Active Drive
- Changing the Active Directory
- Selecting Files
- Viewing Multiple Directories/Drives
- Copying Files
- Moving Files
- Deleting Files
- Creating Directories
- Deleting Directories
- Running a Program through the DOS Shell

STARTING THE DOS SHELL

Why Use the DOS Shell?

When you first turn on your computer, unless someone has kindly set up your startup file to run a program, you're faced with the boring and cryptic DOS prompt. Many beginners find the DOS Shell easier and more friendly, because of its graphical look. With the DOS Shell, you don't have to remember any commands. Instead, you can select commands from menus. The DOS Shell also allows you to use a mouse; the regular DOS screen does not.

Starting the DOS Shell

1. At the DOS prompt, type **DOSSHELL**.

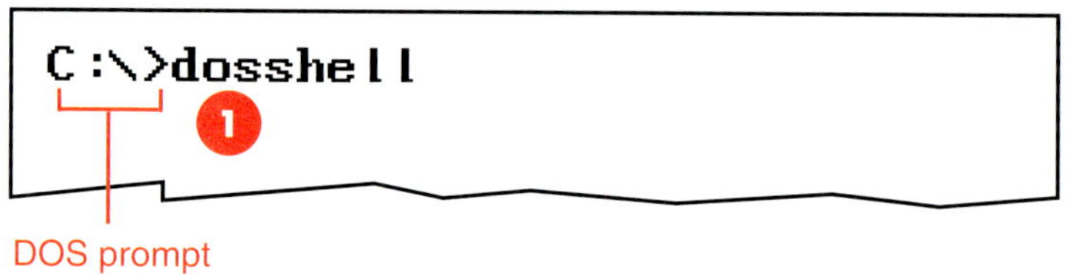

2. Press **Enter**.

LEARNING THE LINGO

DOS prompt: A group of characters on the left side of the screen, followed by a blinking underline. The DOS prompt indicates that DOS is ready to receive your next command.

DOS Shell: A graphics-based program that lets you work with colorful menus and prompts rather than the regular DOS screen.

Graphical environment: A program that includes boxes, pictures, and other shapes in addition to plain text. Sometimes called a *graphical interface.*

UNDERSTANDING THE DOS SHELL SCREEN

Why Learn the Parts of the DOS Shell?

Throughout this book, we'll be referring to various parts of the DOS Shell screen. Take a few minutes to learn them now, so you'll be able to follow along later.

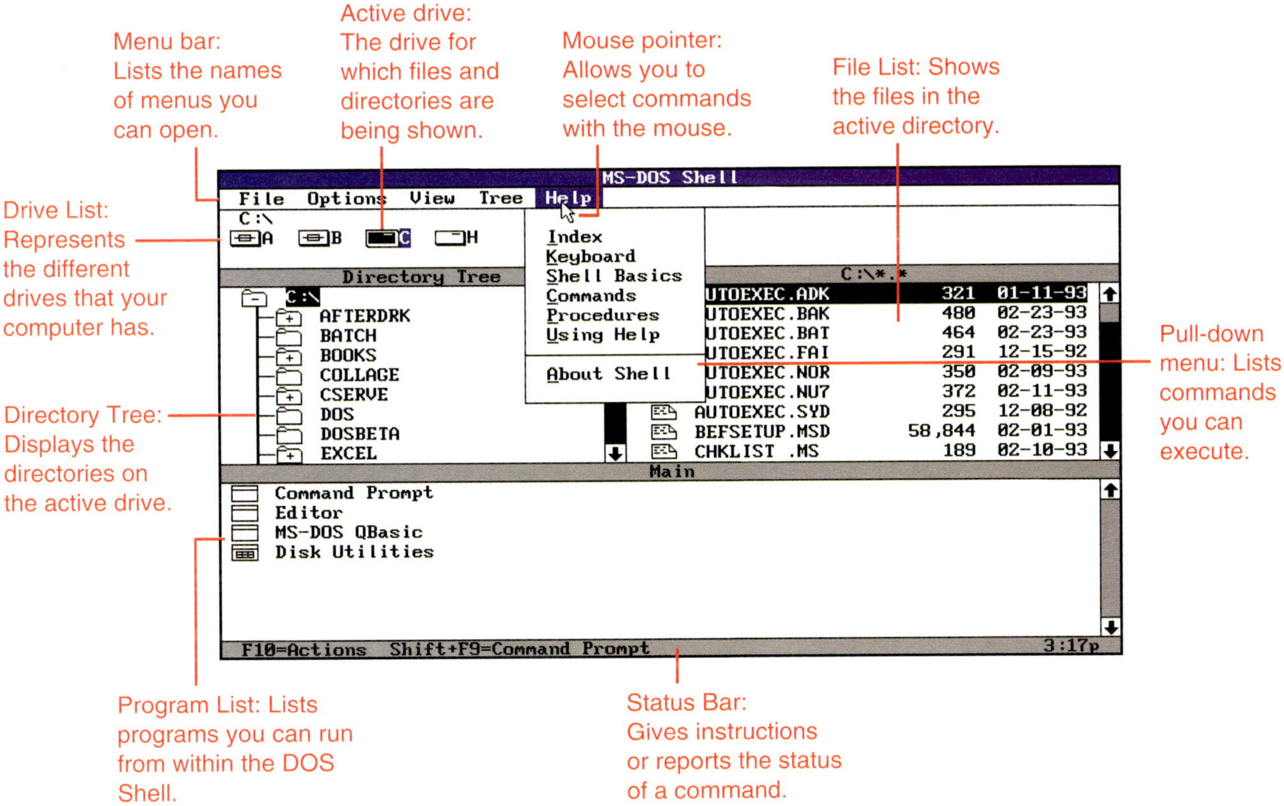

TIP

If your screen looks slightly different, don't worry. In the Selecting Menu Commands task, there will be an exercise in which you will change your screen's display mode to more closely match the one in this book.

LEARNING THE LINGO

Directory: A subsection of a disk. Dividing your disk into directories helps you keep track of files.

Active directory: The directory that DOS is working with at the moment. DOS can work with only one directory at a time.

Drive: A part of your PC that "plays" disks, like your record player plays records. Drives are labeled with letters (A, B, C, and so on).

SELECTING MENU COMMANDS

Why Use DOS Shell Menus?

In the DOS Shell, you select commands from menus to perform useful tasks, such as moving and copying files. You also use menus to get help, to exit the program, and to change the way files, directories, and programs are displayed on-screen.

The DOS Shell's menus are "hidden" in the menu bar. To select a command, you must first open the menu. For example, to select the **M**ove command, you would open the **F**ile menu (where the **M**ove command resides), and then select **M**ove.

You can select commands with either the keyboard or the mouse. Experiment with both to determine which you prefer.

Selecting a Menu Command

1. Point and click on a menu name in the menu bar with the mouse. Or press **F10** on the keyboard, and then type the underlined or highlighted letter in the command name.
2. Click on the command name with the mouse. Or type the underlined or highlighted letter in the name.

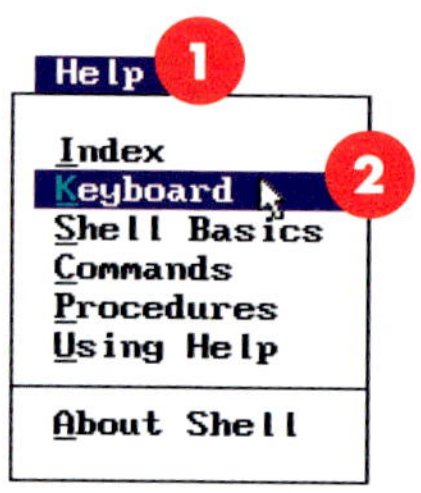

LEARNING THE LINGO

Point: To position the mouse pointer on-screen so its tip touches an item.

Click: To click on something, position the mouse pointer over the item, then press and release the left mouse button once quickly.

TIP

You can use Alt instead of F10; they both work the same. Alt is used in many programs as the key that activates the menu system, so learning to use Alt rather than F10 may prepare you better for learning other programs.

USING DIALOG BOXES

When Do You Use Dialog Boxes?

Some commands open dialog boxes before performing an action. A *dialog box* is a request for additional information your computer needs to perform the command or task you are requesting. You fill in the required information and then choose **OK** to continue executing the command.

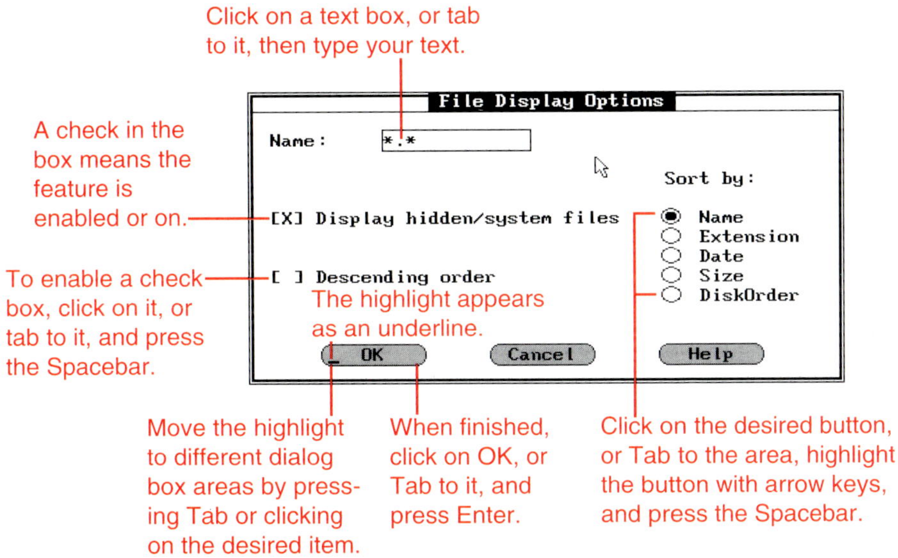

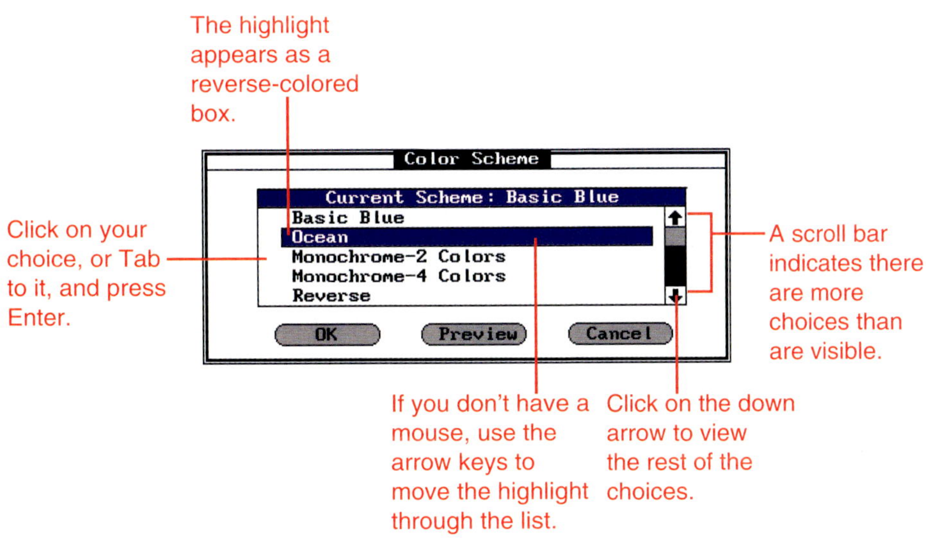

USING DIALOG BOXES

Exercise

This exercise will help you practice using dialog boxes. The DOS Shell can run in several screen modes. The program works the same in all modes, but the screen "look and feel" is different.

The screens in this book are shown in a *graphics mode*, which is more attractive than a *text mode*. Your DOS Shell screen is probably in a text mode right now, because that's its "factory setting." To change to a graphics mode, do the following:

1. Click on **O**ptions on the menu bar, or press **Alt+O**.

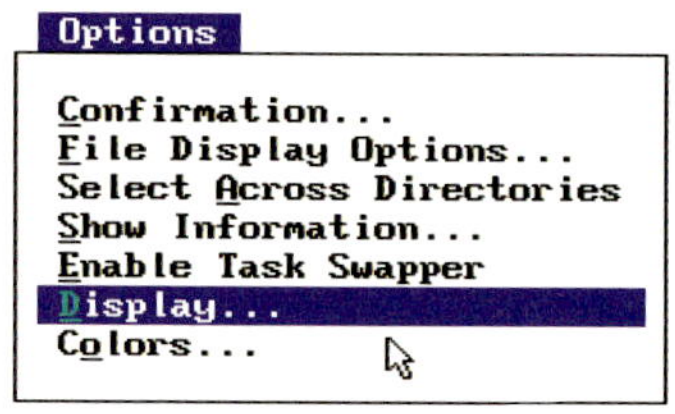

2. Click on the **D**isplay command on the **O**ptions menu, or press **D**.

3. Click on the entry for **Graphics, 25 lines, Low Resolution** to highlight it. Or use the arrow keys to move the highlight to it.

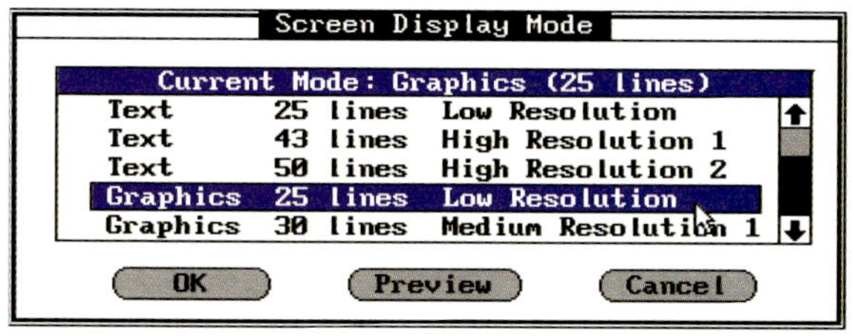

4. Click on **OK**, or press **Enter**.

LEARNING THE LINGO

Graphics mode: A way of displaying a program on-screen that includes graphics (that is, pictures, boxes, and other elements besides text). Graphics mode is attractive but some older monitors cannot use it.

Text mode: A way of displaying a program on-screen so that text and very basic lines are used to simulate pictures. Text mode is a bit drab, but it's speedy, and all monitors can use it.

MOVING THE CURSOR BETWEEN SCREEN AREAS

Why Move Between Screen Areas?

There are several areas of the DOS Shell screen. Many times, to execute a command, the cursor must be in a certain area of the screen. The area the cursor is in is called the *active area*. When an area is active, its title bar is darkened. (If you use the default colors, it's dark blue.)

Moving Between Screen Areas

Keyboard steps:

You can use either of these methods with the keyboard.

A Press **Tab** to move clockwise through the areas.

OR

B Hold down **Shift**, and press **Tab** to move counterclockwise through the areas.

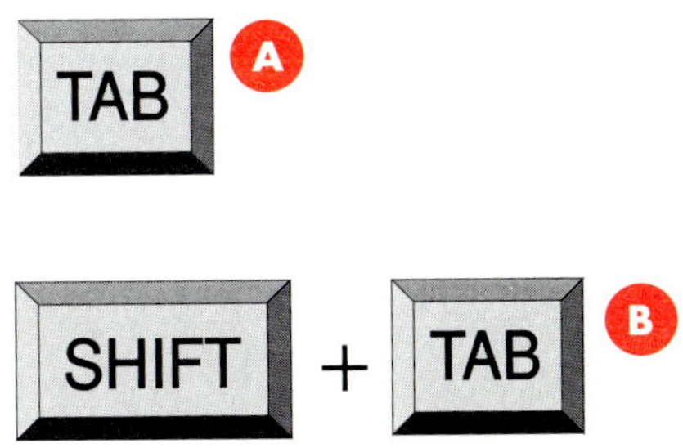

Mouse steps:

To move from area to area using the mouse, simply click on the command, directory, file, or area you want. Its area will immediately become active.

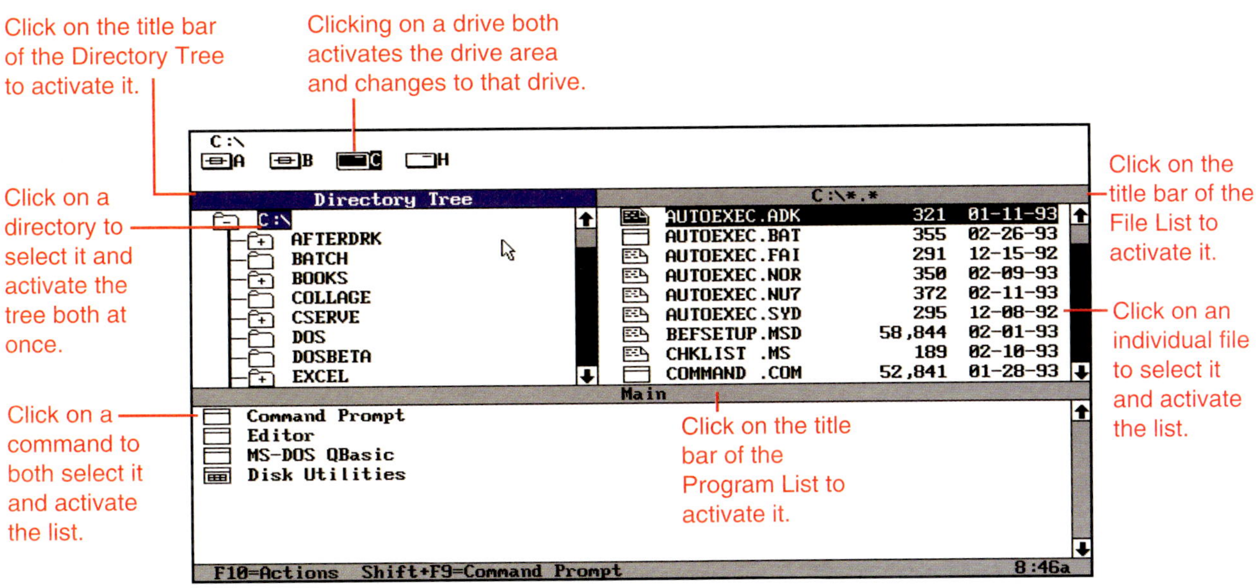

MOVING THE CURSOR BETWEEN SCREEN AREAS

Exercise

This exercise lets you practice activating various screen areas. Later in the book, when you need to activate an area before you can perform a task, you'll be glad you mastered this basic skill.

1. Click anywhere within the Directory Tree area, or press **Tab** until the area becomes highlighted.
2. Click anywhere within the File List area, or press **Tab** until the area becomes highlighted.
3. Click on one of the drive letters at the top of the screen to activate the Drive List, or press **Tab** or **Shift+Tab** until that area is highlighted.

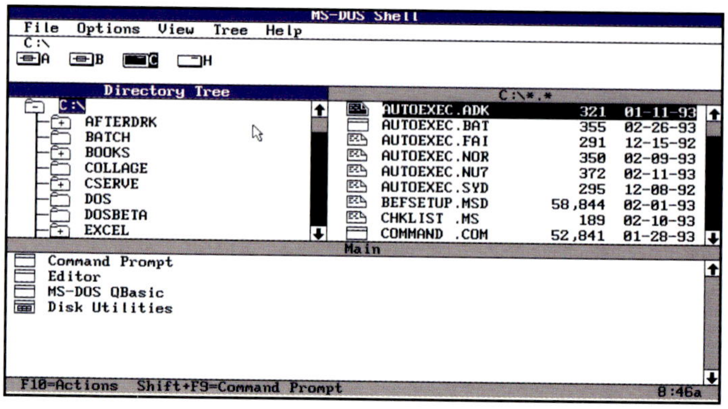

TIP

Keyboard users have something else to worry about: pressing the arrow keys has different effects in different areas.

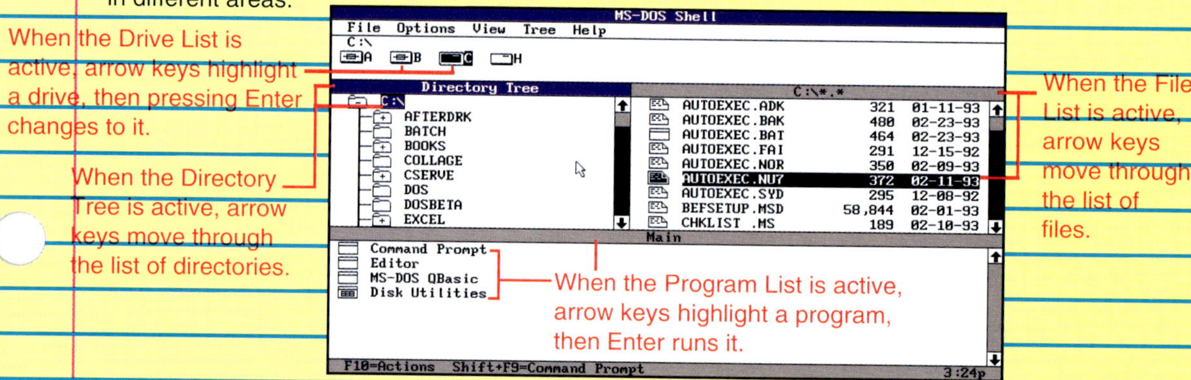

LEARNING THE LINGO

Cursor: The highlight or underline on-screen that tells you "where you are."

Active area: The area of the screen where the cursor is currently located. You can quickly spot the active area because it changes color or shading.

CHANGING THE ACTIVE DRIVE

What Is the Active Drive, and Why Change It?

The *active drive* is the drive for which DOS Shell is currently displaying information. The DOS Shell shows files and directories for only one drive at a time. Yours probably shows drive C now. If you want to see what's on another drive, for example a floppy disk, you must change the active drive.

LEARNING THE LINGO

Directory: A subscription of a disk. Dividing your disk into directories helps you keep track of files. Files with a similar purpose or format can be grouped together in directories.

File: A collection of data that DOS keeps organized under a single name. For example, a letter, a spreadsheet, a text editing program, and a setup utility would each be a file. File names have two parts: a main name, up to eight characters, and then an extension, up to three characters. The two parts are separated by a period, for example, FILENAME.EXT.

Active drive: The disk drive for which files and directories are currently showing on-screen.

TIP

If you're changing to a floppy drive, make sure there's a formatted disk in it. If there's not, insert a disk, and close the drive latch, if your drive has one.

QUICK REFRESHER

To activate a screen area with the keyboard, press **Tab** until the area is highlighted.

Changing the Active Drive

Keyboard steps:

1. Press **Tab** until the drive list is active.

2. Press the right or left arrow key until the desired drive is highlighted.

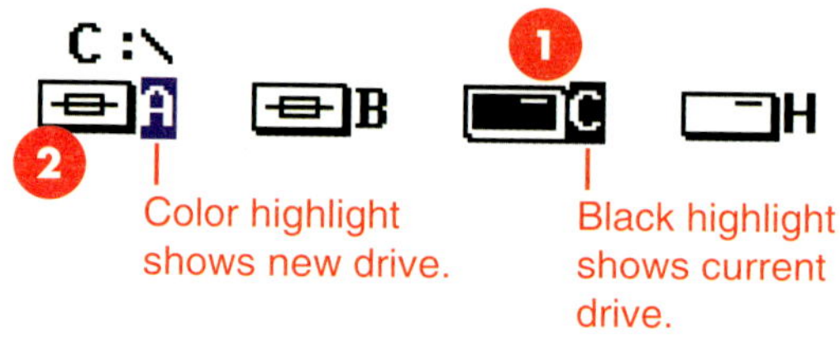

3. Press Enter.

Mouse steps:

1. Click on the desired drive from the drive list.

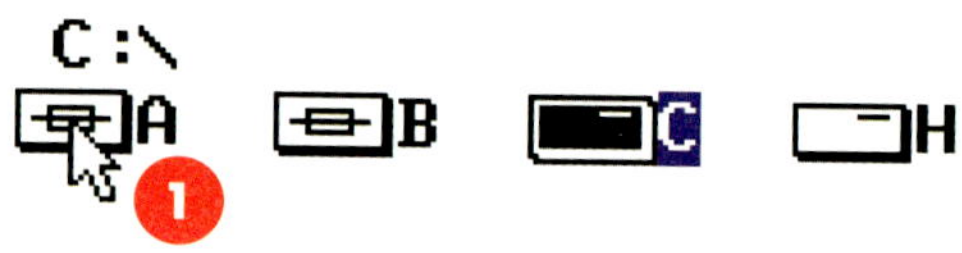

TIP

Here's another way to change the active drive: hold down the **Ctrl** key, and press the letter of the desired drive. For example, to select drive A, press **Ctrl+A**.

CHANGING THE ACTIVE DIRECTORY

Why Change the Active Directory?

The File List shows only one directory's worth of files at a time. It shows the files for the directory whose name is highlighted on the Directory Tree. To view the files on the File List from a different directory, you must highlight a different directory on the Directory Tree.

Changing the Active Directory

Keyboard steps:

1. Press **Tab** until the Directory Tree is active.

2. Use the up and down arrow keys to highlight the desired directory.

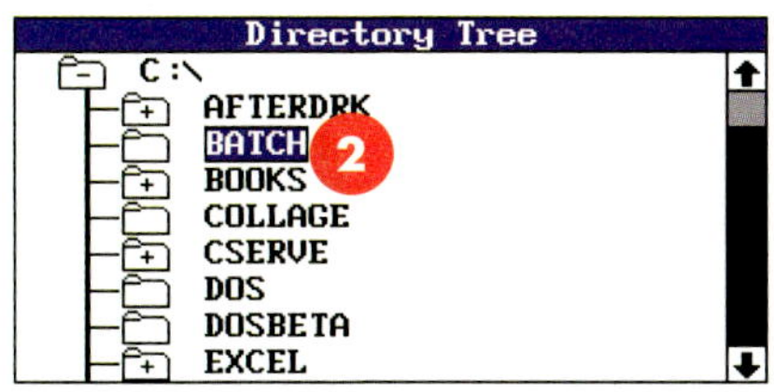

Mouse steps:

1. Click on the desired directory. If the directory you want is not showing, click on the arrows of the scroll bar to bring it into view.

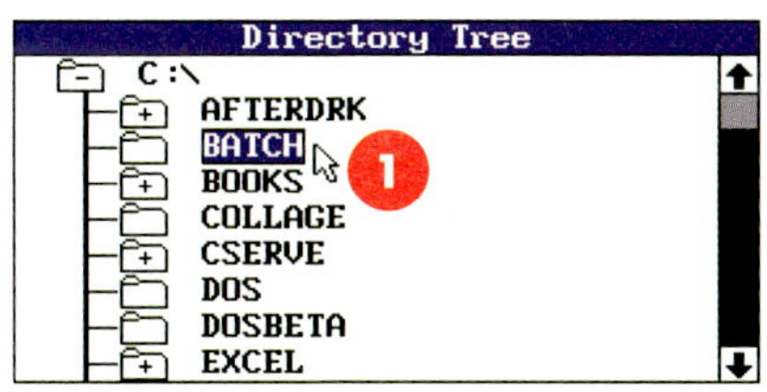

TIP

If you're having trouble picturing what a directory is—picture a huge gymnasium; that's your disk. Now picture movable partitions that section off the gym floor into offices. Each office is a directory. Directories help you keep track of your files; you don't have to search the whole disk for one little file if you remember in which directory you put it.

CHANGING THE ACTIVE DIRECTORY

Exercise

The DOS program files are kept in a special directory, usually called DOS, on drive C. Follow these steps to activate that directory.

1. If drive C is not the active drive, click on it, or press **Ctrl+C**.

2. Click on the DOS directory on the Directory Tree, or **Tab** until the Directory Tree area is active and then use the arrow keys to highlight the DOS directory.

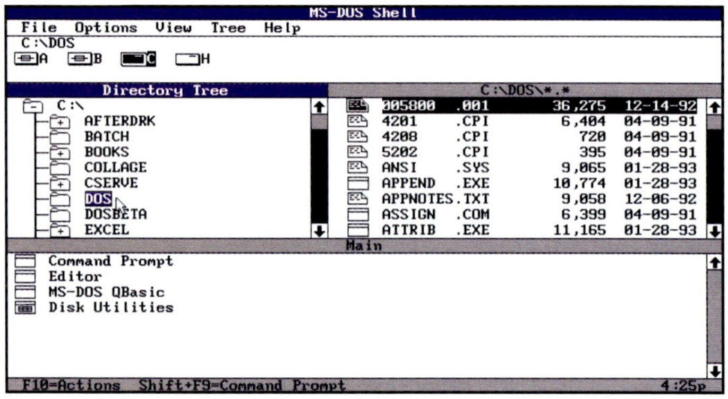

Now that the DOS directory is active, its files appear in the file list.

LEARNING THE LINGO

Directory: A subsection of a disk. Dividing your disk into directories helps you keep track of files. Files with a similar purpose or format can be grouped together in directories.

Active directory: The directory that DOS is working with at the moment. DOS can work with only one directory at a time. The directory whose name is highlighted on the Directory Tree. The active directory's files appear on the File List.

TIP

If the tree is longer than the Directory Tree area can show, don't worry. When the highlight reaches the bottom of the display, the rest of the tree scrolls up into view, line by line, as you continue to press the down arrow key.

SELECTING A SINGLE FILE

Why Select a File?

Before you can act on a file (copy it, move it, delete it, and so on), you have to select it. Just like anything else that you select in the DOS Shell, when a file is selected, it's highlighted.

Selecting a Single File

1. Click anywhere within the **File List**, or press **Tab** until the File List is active.

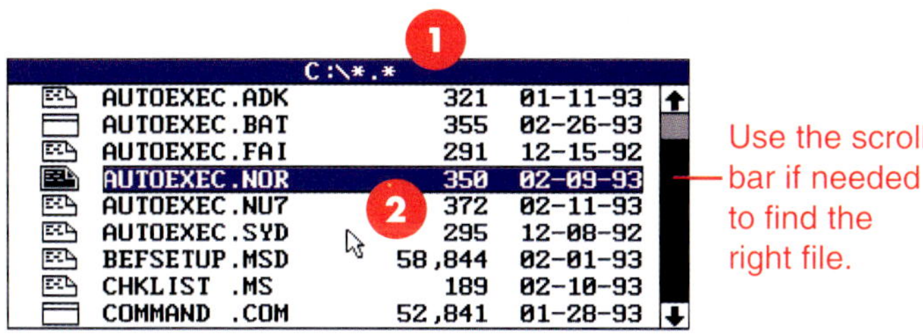

2. Click on the file or press the up or down arrow keys to highlight the file.

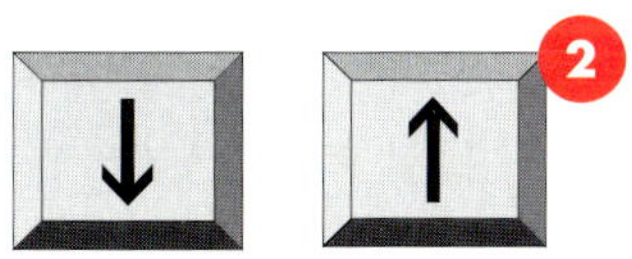

LEARNING THE LINGO

File: A collection of data that DOS keeps organized under a single name. For example, a letter, a spreadsheet, a text editing program, and a setup utility would each be a file. File names have two parts: a main name, up to eight characters, and then an extension, up to three characters. The two parts are separated by a period, for example, FILENAME.EXT.

SELECTING MORE THAN ONE FILE

Selecting Files that are Grouped Together

1. Select the first file of the group, as just described in "Selecting a Single File."

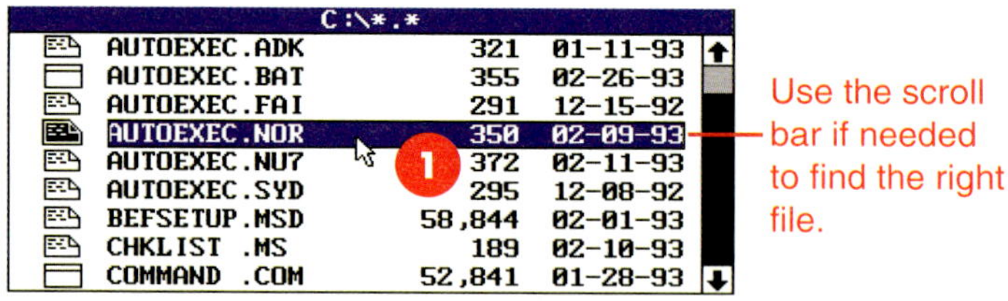

2. Hold down the **Shift** key.

3. Press the up or down arrow keys to highlight additional files, or click on the last file you want to select.

4. Release the **Shift** key.

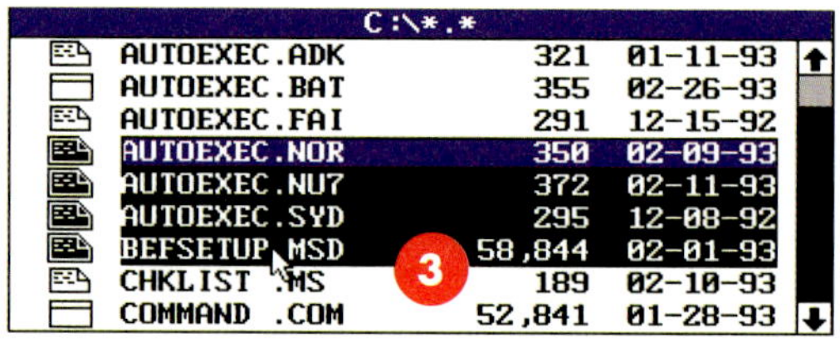

QUICK REFRESHER

Remember, a file extension is a file's letters or numbers after the period in its name. For example, in CONFIG.SYS, SYS is the extension.

TIP

You can also select all the files in the directory using the other methods you've learned for selecting several files. The Ctrl+/ method is the easiest, though.

Selecting Files that Are Not Grouped Together

Mouse steps:

1. Select the first file, as described in "Selecting a Single File."

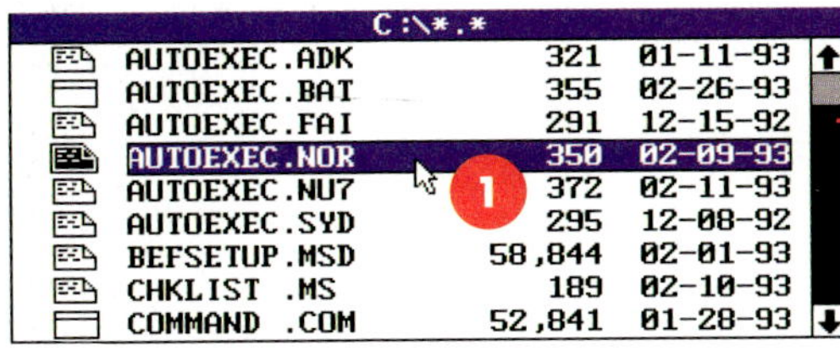

2. Hold down the **Ctrl** key.
3. Click on the next file you want to select.

4. Continue clicking on files until all files you need are selected.
5. Release the **Ctrl** key.

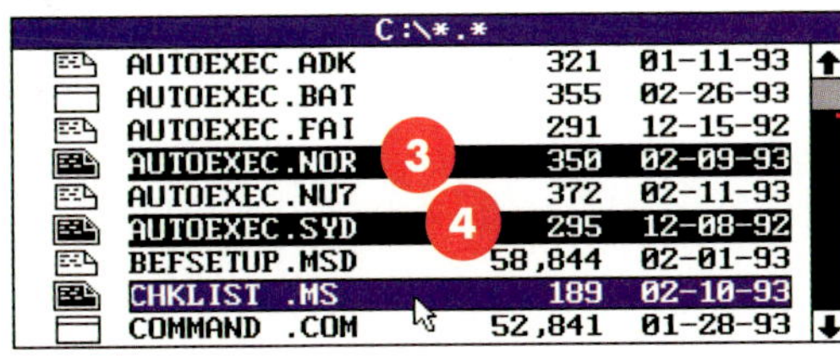

TIP

What do you do with the files now that they're selected? See the sections on "Moving Files," "Copying Files," and "Deleting Files" for some ideas.

To deselect a file while you're in the middle of selecting, select it again (that is, click on it again, or highlight it again and press the space bar). After you've stopped selecting (i.e. released the Ctrl key or pressed Shift+F8 again), selecting something else cancels your current selection.

SELECTING MORE THAN ONE FILE

Keyboard steps:

1. Select the first file, as described in "Selecting a Single File."

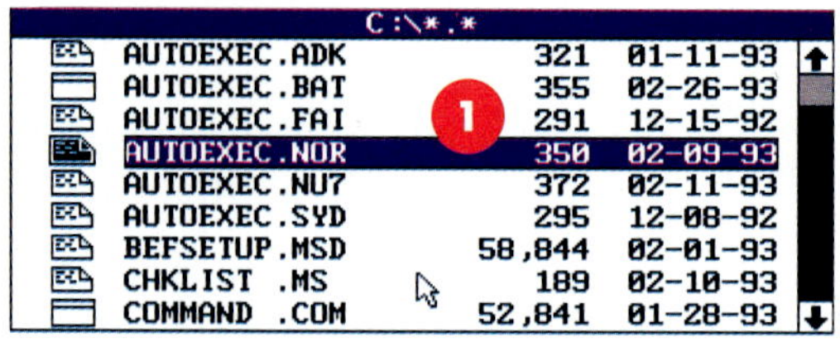

2. Hold down the **Shift** key, and press the **F8** key. This turns on ADD mode.

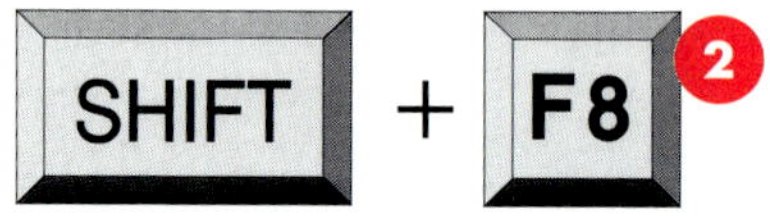

3. Use the arrow keys to highlight the next file to be selected.

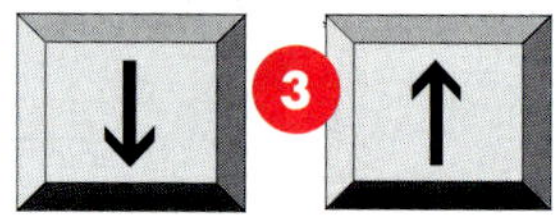

4. Press the **Spacebar** to select the file.

5. Repeat steps 3 and 4 until you're finished; then press **Shift+F8** again to return to normal mode.

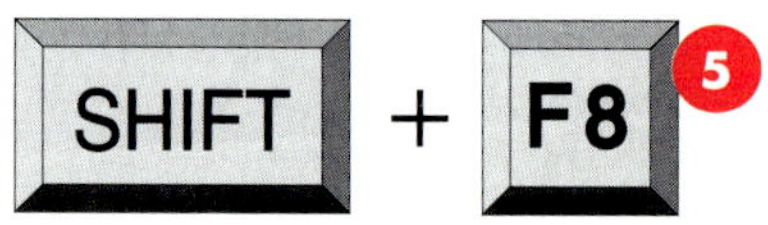

TIP

To select all the files in a directory, click anywhere within the File List, or press **Tab** until the File List is active. Then hold down the **Ctrl** key, and press the / (slash) key.

Exercise

In this exercise, you'll find all the files in the DOS directory that have a file extension of SYS and select them. This will help you practice finding and selecting files.

1. Click on the DOS directory in the Directory Tree, or press Tab to activate the Directory Tree area and then use the arrow keys to highlight the DOS directory.

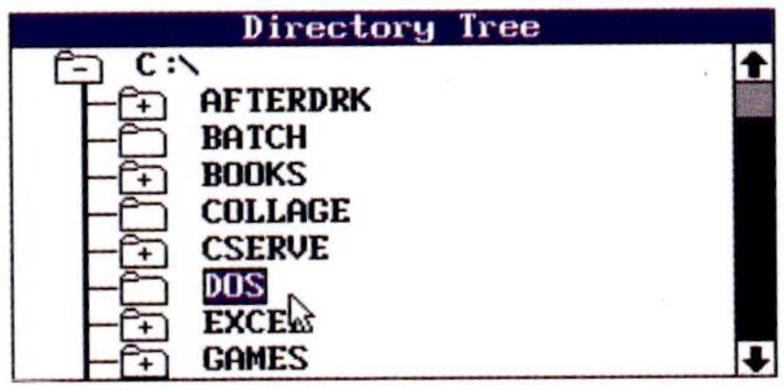

2. Click on the first file you see on the File List that ends in .SYS. Click on the arrows of the scroll bar if you need to display different parts of the list. Or, with the keyboard, press **Tab** to activate the File List, then use the arrow keys to highlight the file.

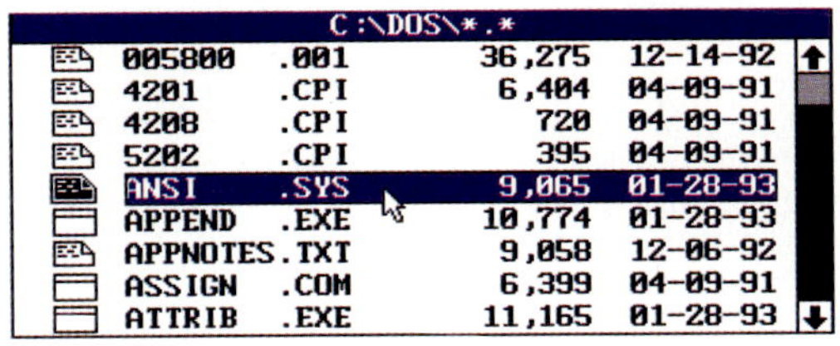

3. If you're using the mouse, hold down the **Ctrl** key. If you're using the keyboard method, press **Shift+F8**.

4. With the mouse, click on the next file that ends in .SYS. (Use the scroll bar, if needed, to locate it.) Or, with the keyboard, use the arrow keys to highlight the next file, then press the spacebar to select it. Repeat until all files that you want have been selected.

5. When you have located and selected all the files that end in .SYS, release the **Ctrl** key (mouse users) or press **Shift+F8** again (keyboard users).

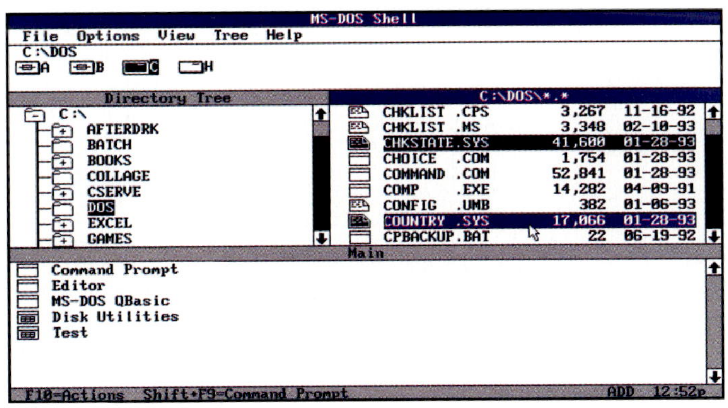

MOVING FILES

Why Move Files?

No matter how carefully you plan when you store a file, eventually you will want it stored somewhere else. You might move an important file into its own directory (see "Creating a Directory"), or move a backup file onto a floppy disk for storage.

TIP

If you have a mouse, you can move files by dragging them from one file list to another.

1. Open the **V**iew menu.
2. Choose **D**ual File Lists.
3. In the top Directory Tree, highlight the directory containing the file(s) you want to move.
4. If you want to move the files to a different drive, select the new drive in the bottom Drive List.
5. In the bottom Directory Tree, highlight the directory where you want the files to go.
6. In the top File List, highlight the files you want to move.
7. Holding down the mouse button, drag the files from the top File List to the desired directory in the bottom directory tree.
8. Select **Yes** when asked if you're sure.

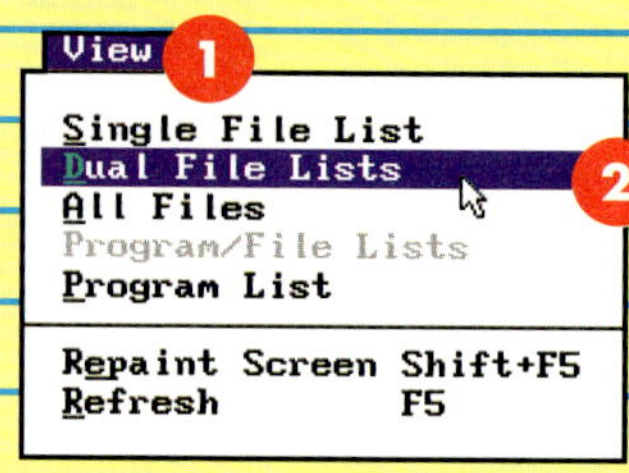

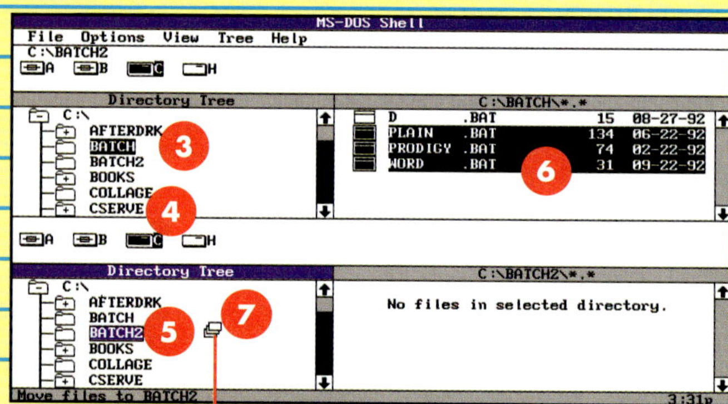

Mouse pointer changes to a stack of "files."

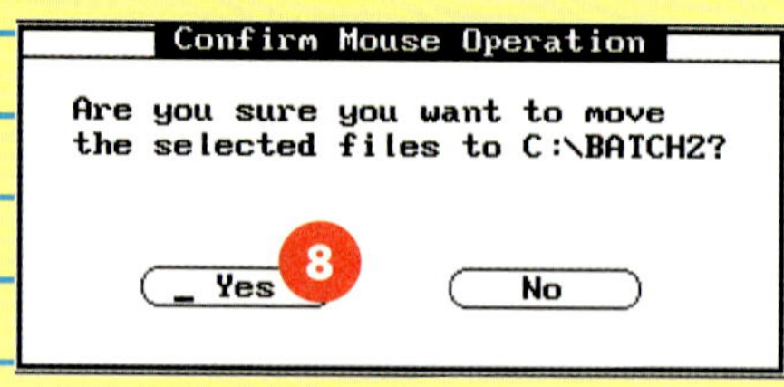

Moving Files

1. Select the files you want to move.

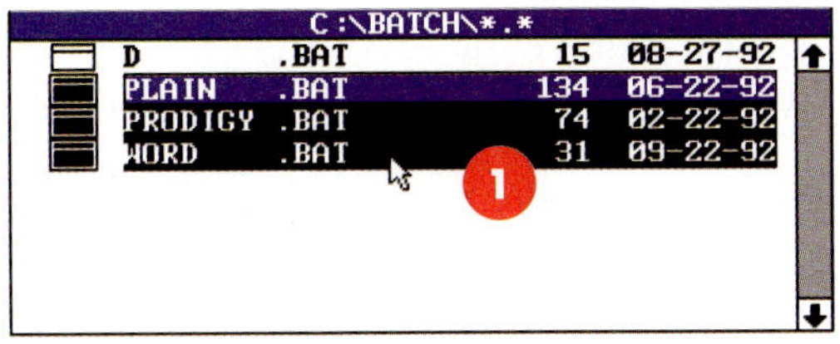

2. Open the **File** menu.
3. Select **Move**.

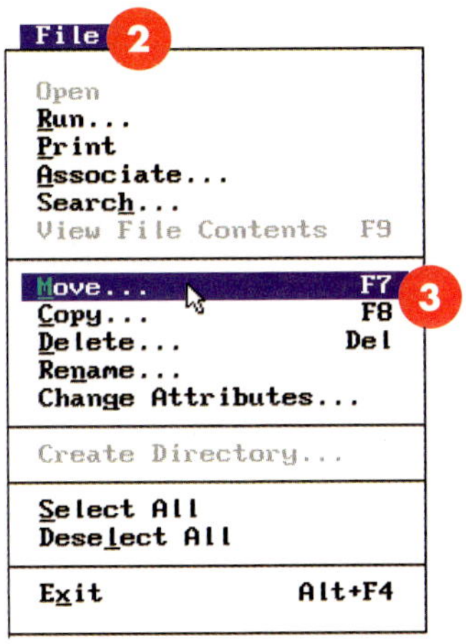

4. In the To box, type the drive and directory where you want the files to go. If you want the file to be renamed, type the new name, too.
5. Select **OK**, or press **Enter**.

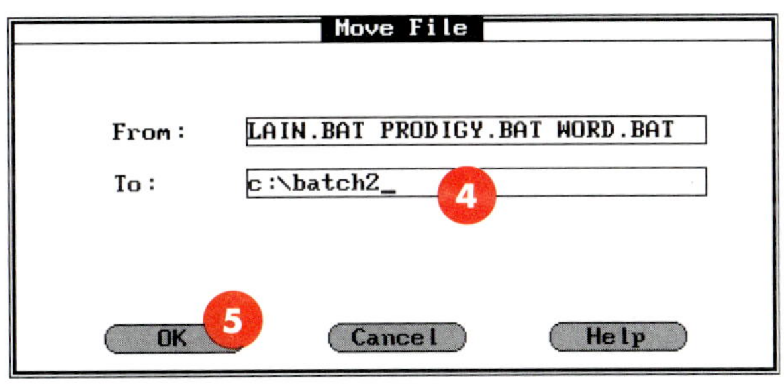

TIP

Instead of steps 2 and 3, you can just press **F7**.

QUICK REFRESHER

To select a single file, just highlight it. To select several contiguous files, hold down the **Shift** key while you select the first and last files in the group. To select several files that are not contiguous, hold down the **Ctrl** key, and click on each one. Or press **Shift+F8**, and then highlight each file, and press the **Spacebar** to select it.

MOVING FILES

Exercise

In this exercise, you'll move the README.TXT file from your DOS directory to your root directory (C:\).

1. Make the **DOS** directory the active directory on the Directory Tree.

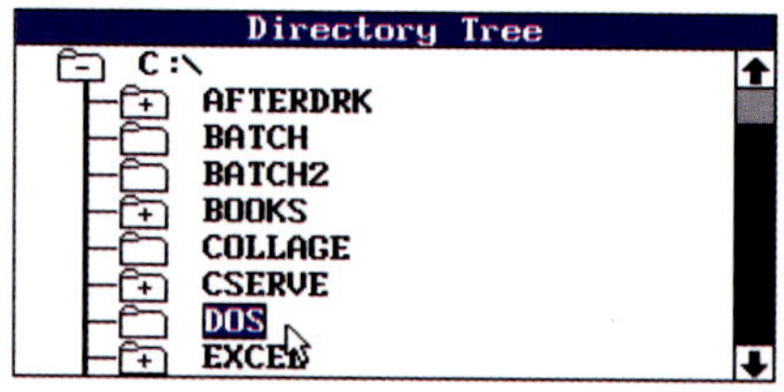

2. Highlight the **README.TXT** file in the File List. (You may have to scroll through the list to find it.)

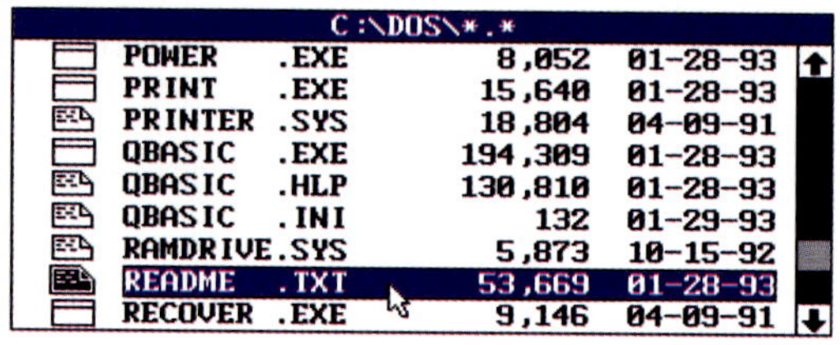

3. Open the **F**ile menu.
4. Select **M**ove.

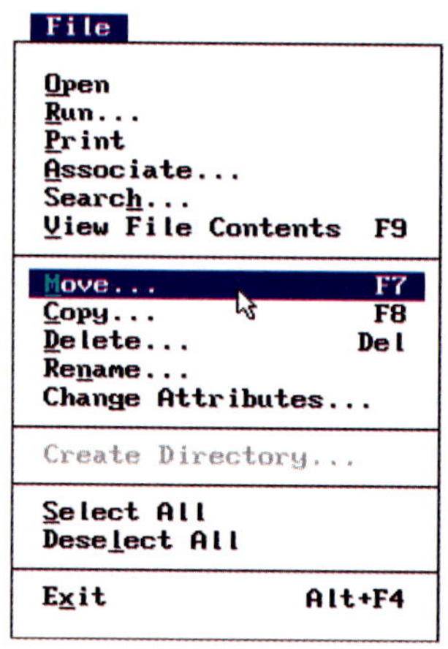

5. In the To box, type **C:**.
6. Select **OK**, or press **Enter**.

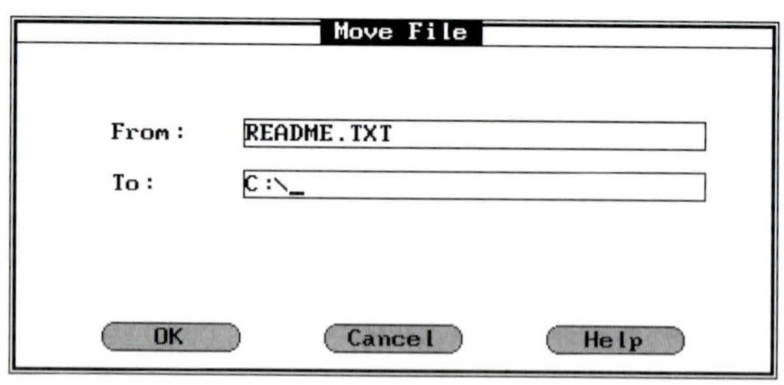

TIP

Move the README.TXT file back into the DOS directory by repeating these steps. In step 1, move to the root directory (the top of the Directory Tree), and in step 5, type **C:\DOS**.

TIP

When you're done, you will probably want to restore the display to a normal view. Open the **V**iew menu again, and choose Program/**F**ile Lists.

QUICK REFRESHER

To highlight a file, first activate the File List area. Then use the arrow keys to move the highlight through the list, or use the scroll bar to move the desired file into view and then click on it.

COPYING FILES

Why Copy Files?

People copy files because they realize that accidents can happen. For example, you might copy the accounting files onto a floppy disk and store the floppy disk in a different building, so in the event of a disaster, the files would be safe. On a much less grand scale, you might simply want to make a copy of a file before you change it, so you'll be able to retain the original.

TIP

If you have a mouse, you can copy files by dragging them from one file list to another.

1. Open the **V**iew menu.
2. Choose **D**ual File Lists.
3. In the top Directory Tree, highlight the directory containing the file(s) you want to move.
4. If you want to copy the files to a different drive, select the new drive in the bottom Drive List.
5. In the bottom Directory Tree, highlight the directory where you want the files to go.
6. In the top File List, highlight the files you want to move.
7. Holding down the mouse button, drag the files from the top File List onto the directory name on the bottom directory tree.
8. Select **Yes** when asked if you're sure.

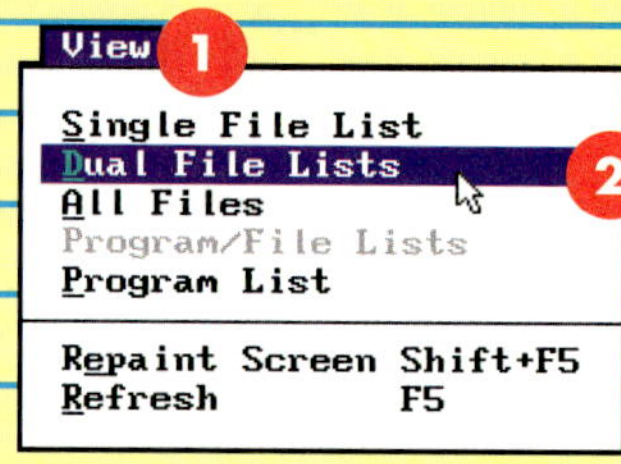

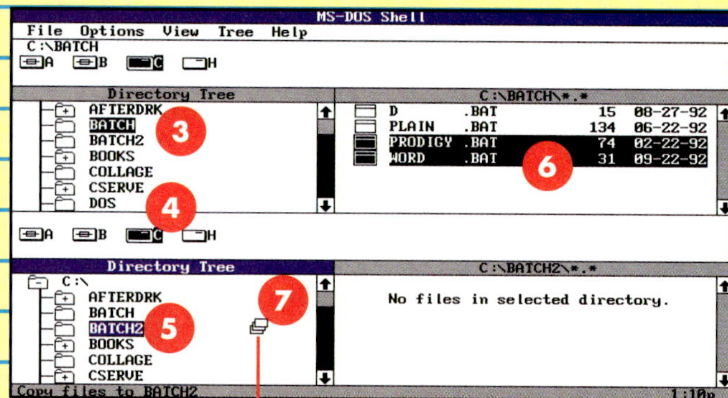

Mouse pointer changes to a stack of "files."

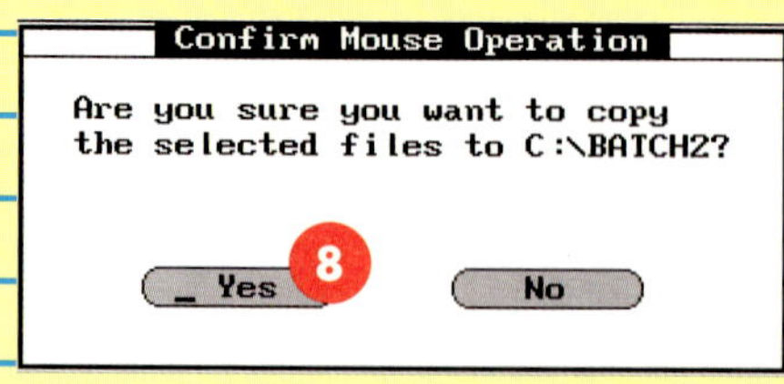

Copying Files

1. Select the files you want to copy.

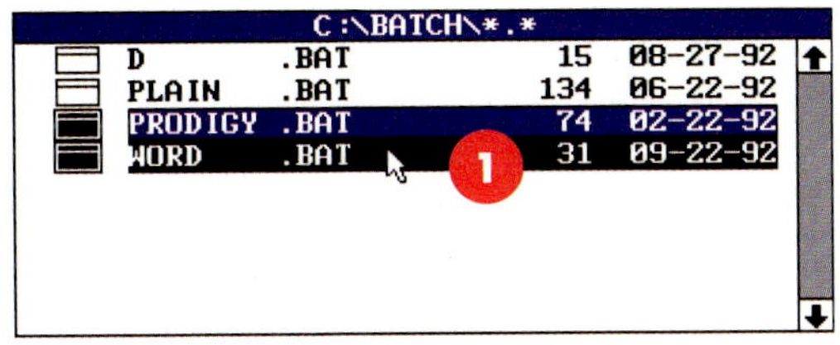

2. Open the **File** menu.
3. Select **Copy**.

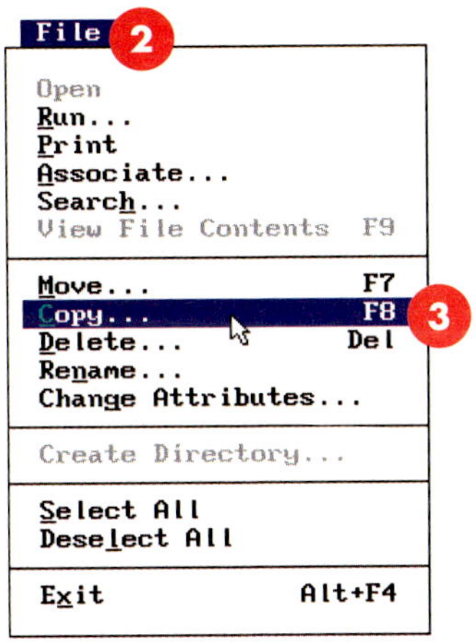

4. In the To box, type the drive and directory where you want the files to go. If you want the copy to have a different name, type it too.
5. Select **OK**, or press **Enter**.

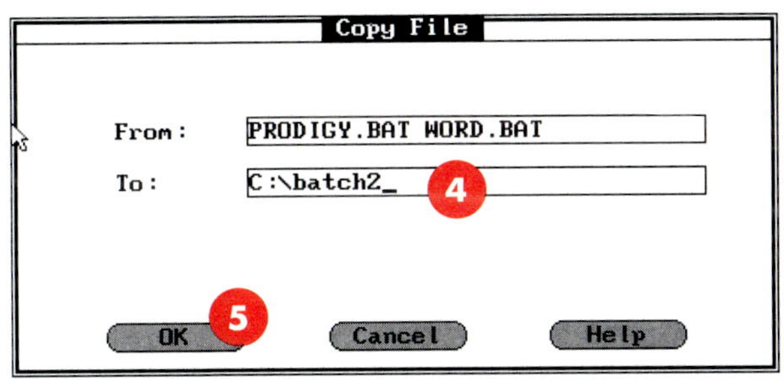

TIP

Instead of steps 2 and 3, you can just press **F8**.

QUICK REFRESHER

To select a single file, just highlight it. To select several contiguous files, hold down the **Shift** key while you select the first and last files in the group. To select several files that are not contiguous, hold down the **Ctrl** key and click on each one. Or press **Shift+F8**, and then highlight each file, and press the **Spacebar** to select it.

COPYING FILES

Exercise

In this exercise, you'll copy the APPNOTES.TXT file from your DOS directory to your root directory (C:\).

1. Make the DOS directory the active directory on the Directory Tree.
2. Highlight the **APPNOTES.TXT** file in the File List. (You may have to scroll through the list to find it.)

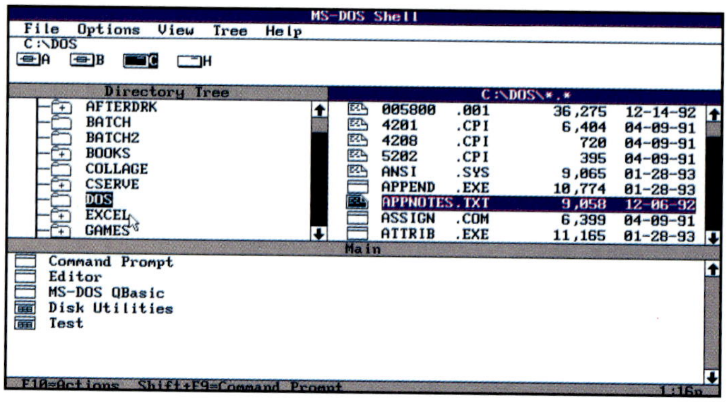

3. Open the **F**ile menu.
4. Select **C**opy.

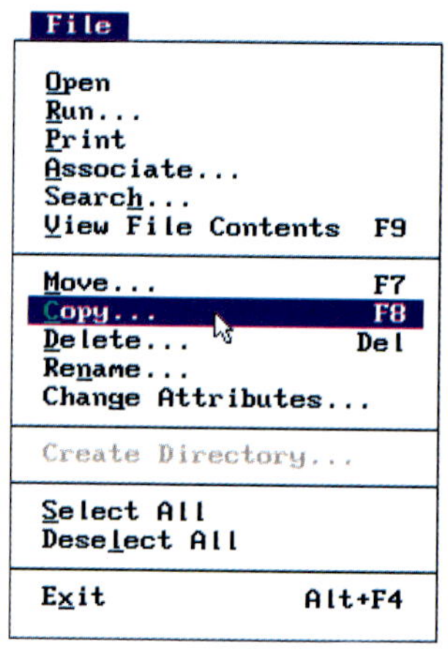

5. In the To box, type **C:**.
6. Select **OK**, or press **Enter**.

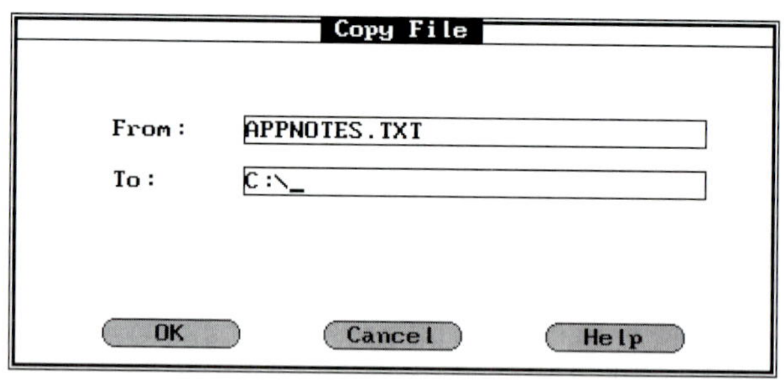

Why Delete Files?

Why delete files? For the same reason that you take out the trash! You delete files that you are done with so they don't clutter up your disk, making it hard for you to find the files that are still valuable. You might also delete a file that contains sensitive information, so someone else using your computer won't see it.

Deleting Files

1. In the File List, select the files you want to delete. (Refer to "Selecting Files" if you're not sure how.)

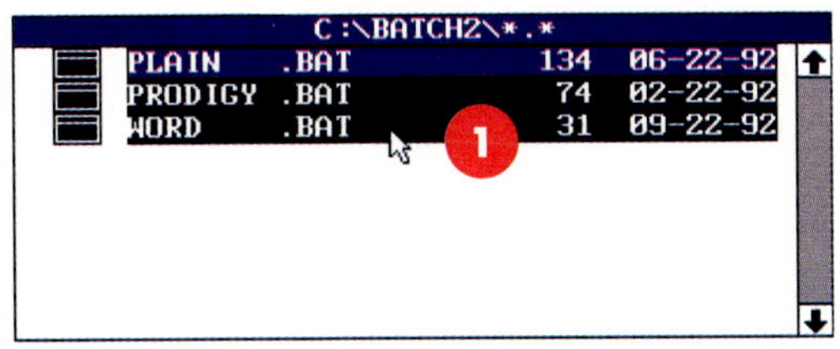

2. Press the **Del** key.

3. Select **OK** to confirm.

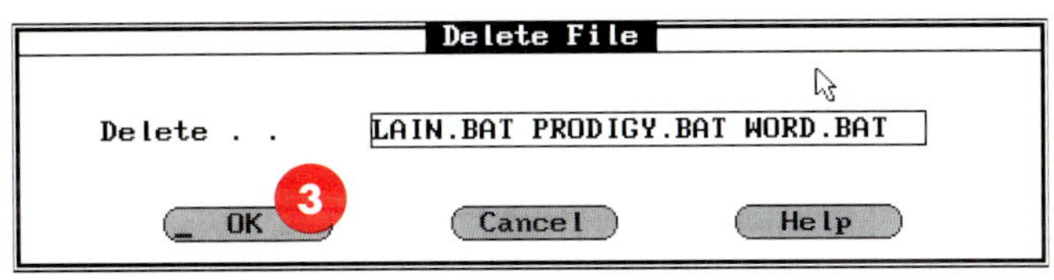

4. If you are deleting multiple files, select **Yes** for each file.

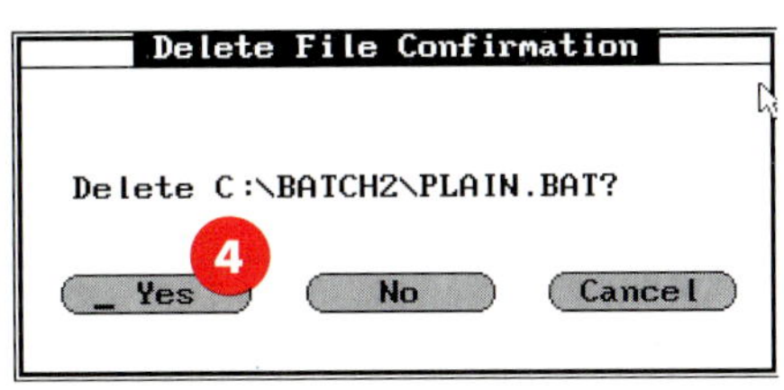

TIP

Instead of step 2, you can open the **F**ile menu and select **D**elete.

DELETING FILES

Exercise

In this exercise, we'll practice both copying and deleting. You'll make a copy of the COMMAND.COM file in your root directory, and then you'll delete the copy.

1. Highlight the root directory (C:\) on the Directory Tree.
2. Highlight the **COMMAND.COM** file on the File List.

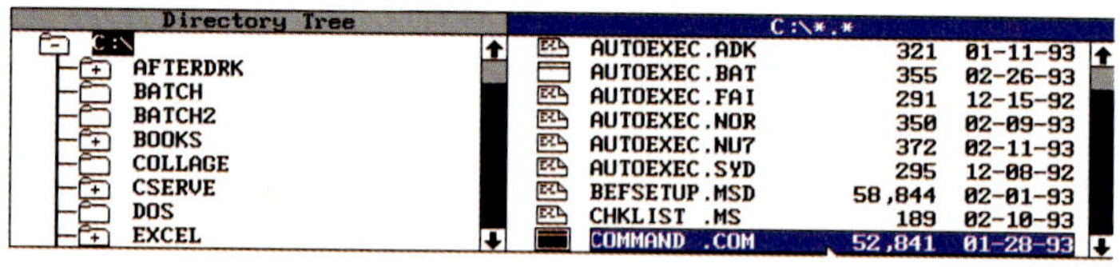

3. Press **F8**.
4. Type **MYCOPY.BAK** in the To box.
5. Select **OK**.

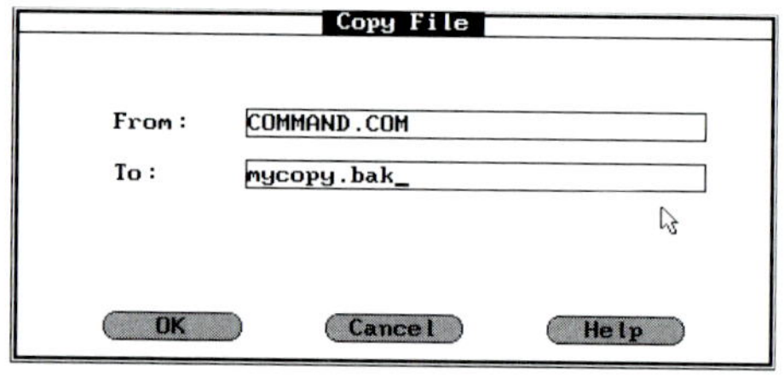

6. Highlight **MYCOPY.BAK** on the File List.
7. Press the **Del** key.

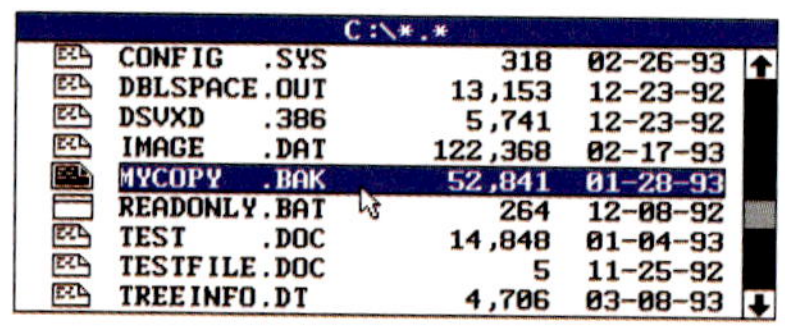

8. Select **Yes**, or press **Enter**.

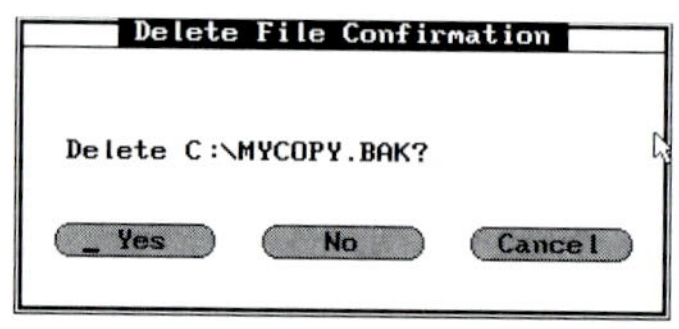

TIP

If you accidentally delete a file, see the "Undeleting Files" task in the Handy DOS 6 Utilities part of the book.

CREATING A DIRECTORY

Why Create a Directory?

Your computer may have come with a couple of directories, such as DOS or WINDOWS. As you install programs, the installation programs may create other directories, too. But if you just have some files that you want to "put somewhere," you might want to create a directory in which to stash them.

When creating a directory, as with real estate, location is everything. A new directory's location depends on what directory is active on the Directory Tree at the time of its creation.

You must activate the directory that the new directory is to be "subordinate to" on the Directory Tree before you begin. For example, if you want a regular directory, such as C:\WORD, highlight C:\ before you start creating WORD. If you want a subdirectory, such as C:\WORD\DATA, then highlight C:\WORD before you start creating DATA.

Creating a Directory

1. Highlight the directory under which the new directory is to appear on the Directory Tree.

2. Open the **File** menu.
3. Select Cr**e**ate Directory.

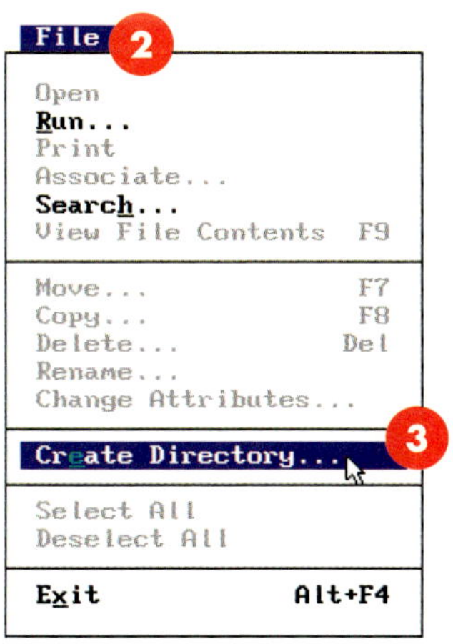

The DOS Shell

CREATING A DIRECTORY

4 Type the name in the New Directory name box.

5 Select **OK**, or press **Enter**.

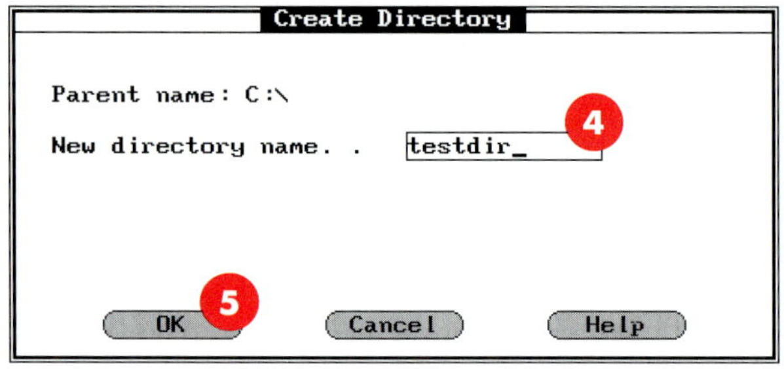

Exercise

In this exercise, you'll practice creating directories by making one called TEST. You'll use it later, in the Deleting a Directory task, to practice deleting directories.

1 Highlight the root directory (**C:**) on the Directory Tree.

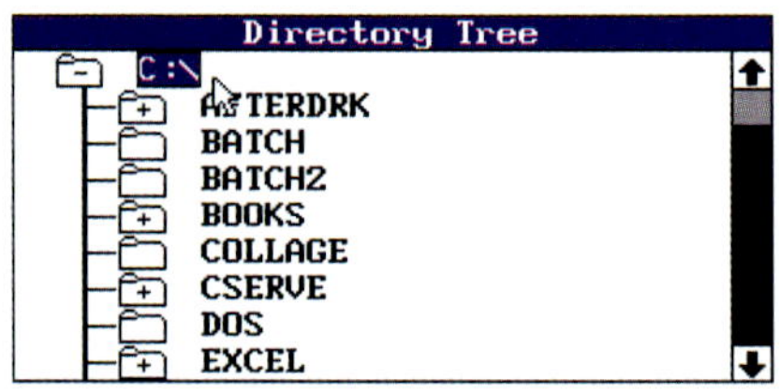

2 Open the **File** menu.

3 Select Create Directory.

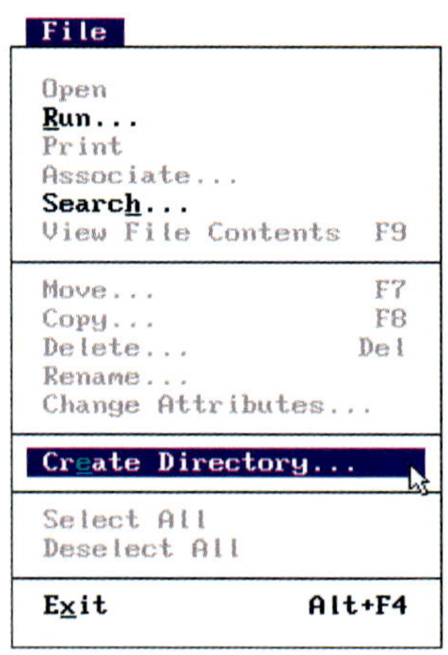

4 Type **TEST**.

5 Select **OK**.

DELETING A DIRECTORY

Why Delete a Directory?

Over time, you may find that you don't use all the directories you create. Or you may want to completely rid your hard disk of an awful software program that you bought but never use.

Before you can delete a directory, you must delete all the files from it. Refer to the "Deleting Files" task. Be careful, however, not to delete any important files or directories!

Deleting a Directory

1. Highlight the directory on the Directory Tree that you want to delete.

2. Press the **Del** key.

3. Select **Yes**, or press **Enter** to confirm.

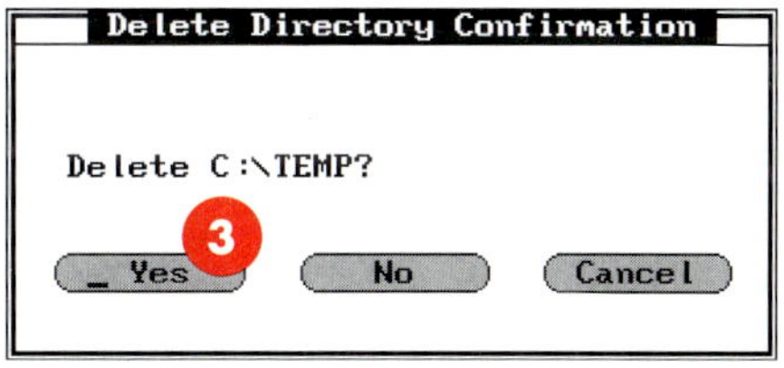

QUICK REFRESHER

To delete a file, highlight it, and press **Del**, then answer **Yes**. To delete several files at once, highlight them all before you press **Del**.

The DOS Shell

DELETING A DIRECTORY

Exercise

You can do this exercise only if you created the TEST directory in the "Creating a Directory" task exercise. If you didn't, go back and do it now before continuing.

1. Highlight the **TEST** directory on the Directory Tree.

2. Press the **Del** key.

3. Select **Yes**.

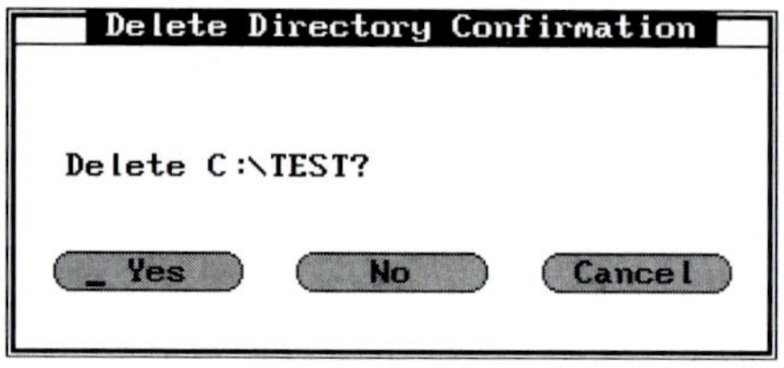

RUNNING A PROGRAM FROM THE DOS SHELL

Why Run a Program from the DOS Shell?

If you use the DOS Shell to manage your files, you may not want to exit from DOS Shell every time you want to run another program. Luckily, you don't have to. There are several ways to run a program from within the DOS Shell: from the File List, from the Program List, and using the Run command.

Running a Program from the File List

1. On the Directory Tree, highlight the directory that contains the program you want to run.

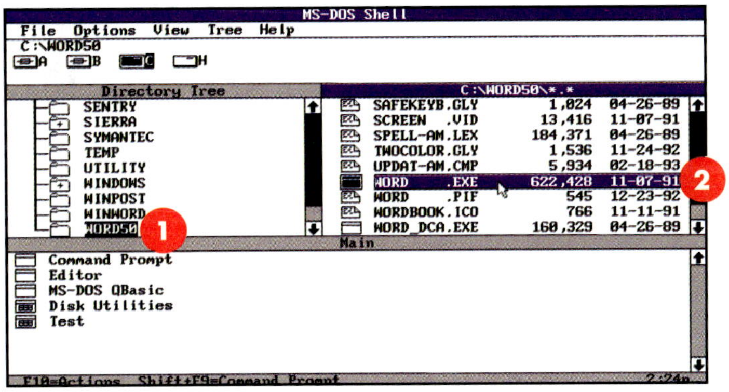

2. On the File List, double-click on the name of the program you want to run, or highlight the name, and press **Enter**.

TIP

How do you tell which of the files is the one that runs the program? Look for files with the same name as what you normally type at the DOS prompt to start the program, with the extension of EXE, COM, or BAT.

LEARNING THE LINGO

Program List: The area of the DOS Shell screen where commonly used programs wait to be run.

Program group: A group of similar programs grouped together on the Program List to better keep track of them.

Program item: The name of a program on the Program List.

Running a Program from the Program List

1. Click on the **Program List** area, or press **Tab** to activate it.

2. If the program you want to run is visible, double-click on it, or highlight it, and press **Enter**.

3. If the program you want to run is in a different program group, double-click on the program group. Or highlight it and press **Enter**, then return to step 2.

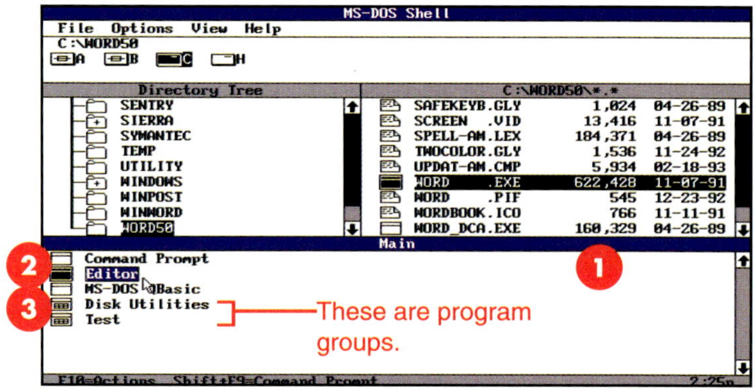

TIP

For example, if you wanted to run Microsoft Word, in step 3, you might type **C:\WORD\WORD.EXE**.

TIP

Another way to run a program is with the **R**un command on the **F**ile menu. To use it, open the **F**ile menu and select **R**un.

Type the complete path and name of the program to run, then select **OK**.

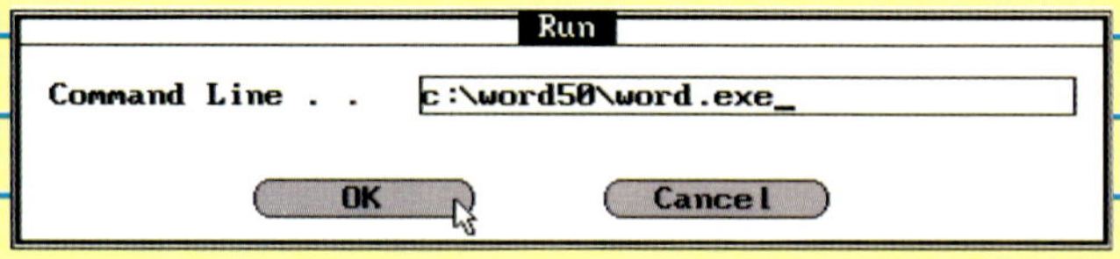

USING THE TEMPORARY COMMAND PROMPT

What is a Temporary Command Prompt?

As you may already have learned, a command prompt (also called the DOS prompt) is an assortment of characters that appear at the left edge of your screen, beckoning you to type a DOS command. When you exit from a program (such as the DOS Shell), you return to the command prompt.

If you are not ready to exit from the DOS Shell but need to issue a quick command or two at the DOS prompt, you can use the *temporary* command prompt. It looks just like the regular DOS prompt in every way, and you can use almost any DOS command at it. However, it's temporary because it "goes away" like a mirage when you type **EXIT** to return to the DOS Shell.

TIP

If you ever forget whether you're at a temporary command prompt or a real one, just type **EXIT** and press **Enter**. Nothing will happen if you're at a real command prompt. It's like pinching yourself to see if you're dreaming!

Using the Temporary Command Prompt

1. Click on the **Program List**, or **Tab** to activate it.

2. If the Main program group is not open, double-click on its icon, or highlight it, and press **Enter**.

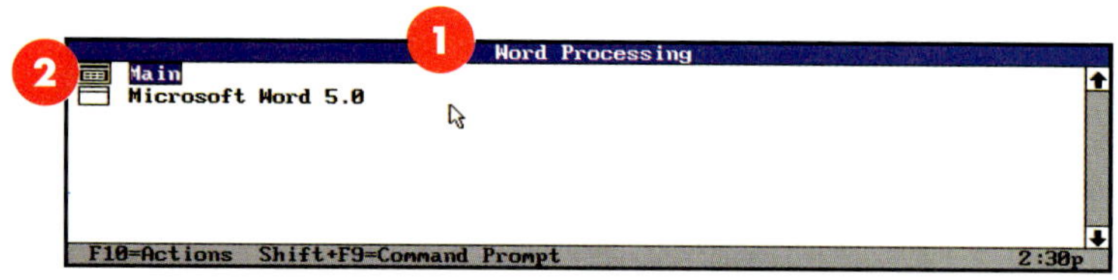

3. Double-click on the words **Command Prompt**, or highlight them, and press **Enter**.

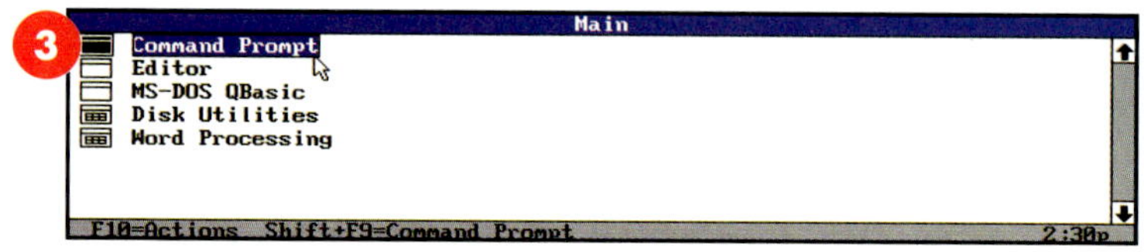

4. Issue your command at the temporary prompt.

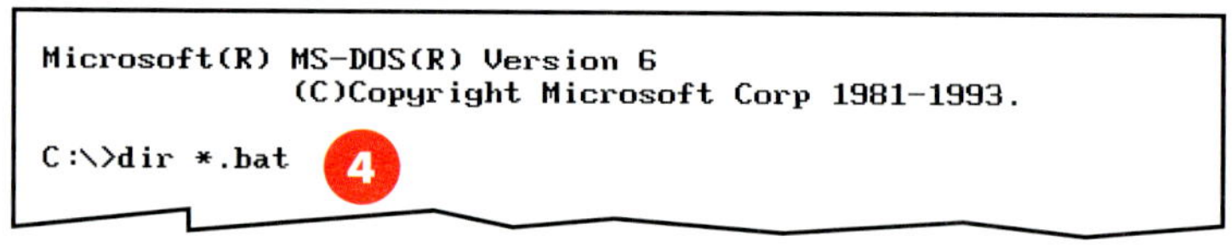

5. When you are finished, type **EXIT** and press Enter to return to the DOS Shell.

EXITING THE DOS SHELL

Why Exit the DOS Shell?

If you're a beginner, you may never need to exit the DOS Shell. However, chances are good that you will eventually need to work from the real DOS prompt, not just the temporary one that DOS Shell provides within itself. For example, if you are installing a new program from floppy disks, you will have best results if you work outside the DOS Shell.

Exiting the DOS Shell

1. Open the **File** menu.
2. Select **Exit**.

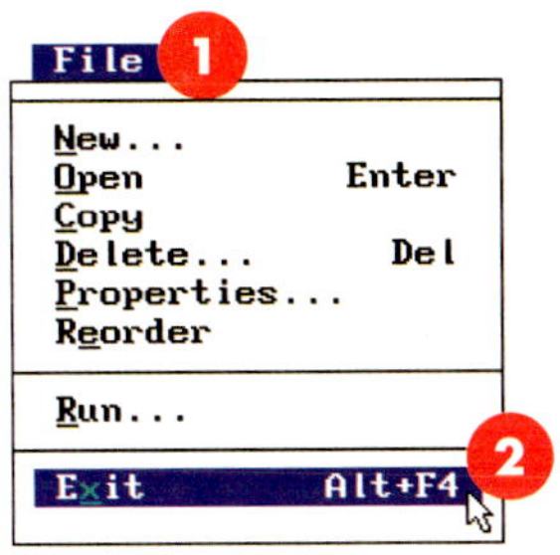

The DOS Shell

PART 2

Working at the DOS Prompt

This section guides you through life at the DOS prompt, that jumble of letters and numbers followed by a seductively blinking underline character. It beckons you to type commands, but how do you know what to type? This section will help you answer that question by guiding you through all of the most common tasks that you might perform at the DOS prompt.

- Understanding the Parts of a DOS Command
- Setting Up Your DOS Prompt
- Changing the Active Drive
- Listing Files in the Active Directory
- Listing Files in a Different Directory
- Listing Only Certain Files
- Sorting a File Listing
- Creating a Directory
- Deleting a Directory
- Copying a File
- Copying Several Files
- Moving a File
- Moving Several Files
- Renaming Files
- Deleting Files
- Setting Up Delete Protection
- Undeleting Files
- Formatting a Disk
- Creating a System Diskette

UNDERSTANDING THE PARTS OF A DOS COMMAND

Why Learn About DOS Commands?

Even though the DOS Shell is a wonderful tool, there will inevitably be times when you must use a plain-old DOS command. For example, if you want to install a new program, you must type its setup command at the DOS prompt—usually SETUP or INSTALL.

As you become more skilled with DOS, you may want to start using the DOS prompt to issue commands that you previously issued through the DOS Shell, because typing at the prompt can be faster.

Before you can use the DOS prompt to issue commands, though, you must understand a few basic facts about DOS commands.

Examining a Typical DOS Command

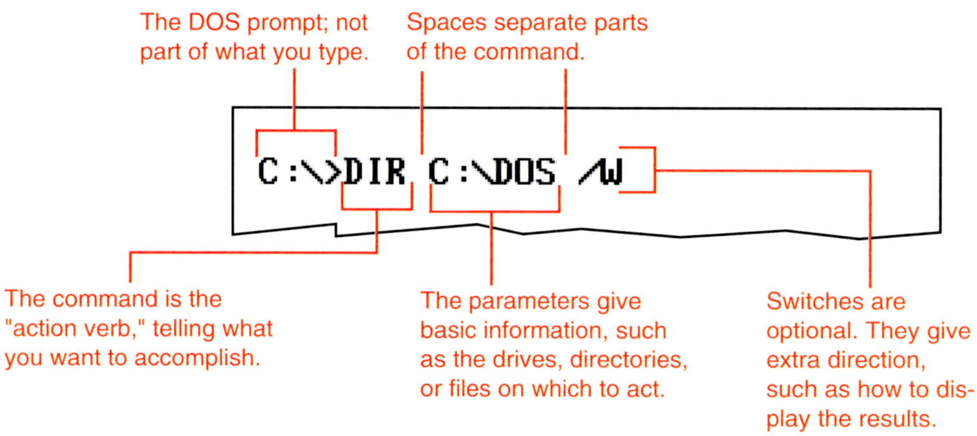

TIP

If your prompt does not show the active drive and directory (for example, if it looks like this: **C>**), stay tuned. The next section will show you how to make yours match the ones in this book.

LEARNING THE LINGO

Command: An "action verb" telling DOS what action you want it to take.

Parameter: Extra information that goes along with a command, telling DOS which drives, directories, or files in which to limit its action.

Switch: An optional specification that directs DOS to process the command in a special way.

Example DOS Commands

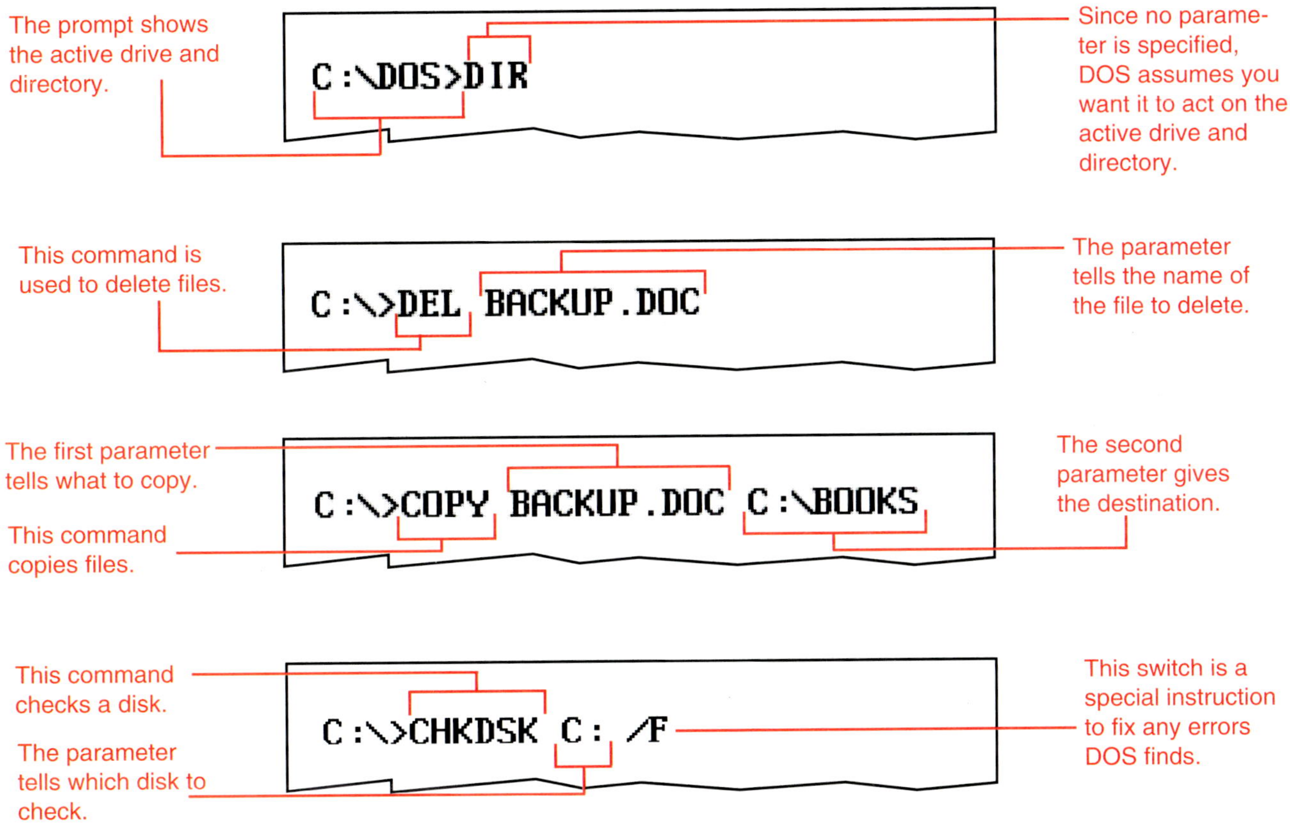

QUICK REFRESHER

Remember, DOS is only aware of one drive and directory at once. In the DOS Shell, the active drive and directory were displayed in the Directory Tree. At the DOS prompt, they are shown as part of the prompt.

TIP

How do you know when to use a parameter or switch? It's easy to skip switches; they're optional. But parameters are more tricky. Sometimes the parameter is required; other times, if you skip the parameter, DOS will assume you want to act on the current drive and directory. Beginners can type **HELP**, followed by the command name to get some assistance (for example, **HELP DIR**).

SETTING UP YOUR DOS PROMPT

Why Set Up Your DOS Prompt?

In the examples in this book, you'll notice that the active drive and directory are always shown as part of the DOS prompt. This is a tremendous help; it's a constant reminder of "where you're at." If your DOS prompt looks like this:

C>

rather than this:

C:\>

then it's not set up to show the active drive and directory. You may not understand the command just yet, but you'll be much happier later if you take the time now to set up your DOS prompt to match the ones shown in this book.

Displaying the Active Drive and Directory at the DOS Prompt

1. Type **PROMPT PG**.

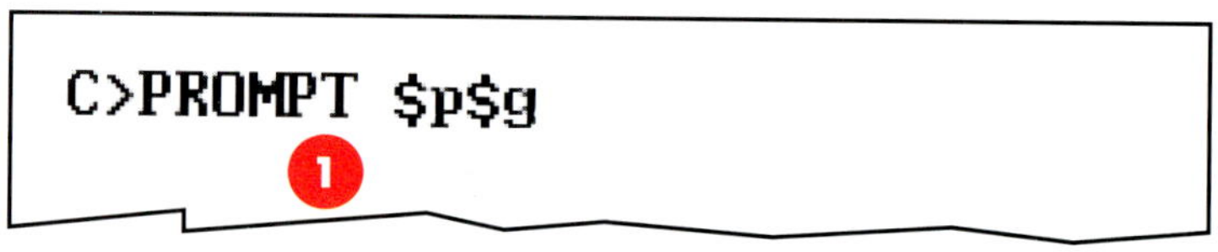

2. Press **Enter**.

TIP

Ask an experienced DOS user to add this command to your startup file (AUTOEXEC.BAT) so that you won't have to issue this command each time you start your computer.

CHANGING THE ACTIVE DRIVE

Why Change the Active Drive?

Your computer system probably has several drives: a hard drive (usually C:), and one or two floppy drives (usually A: and B:). The DOS prompt tells you which drive is active. For example, if your prompt says **C:\DOS>**, then drive C: is active. To work with files on a different drive, you can make the other drive active.

Changing the Active Drive

1. Type the drive letter of the new drive followed by a colon.

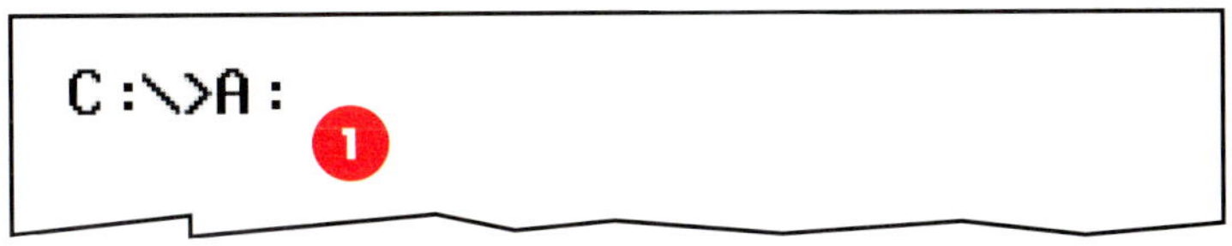

2. Press **Enter**.

TIP

You can work with other drives without making them active, but you must specify them as parameters when issuing the command. For example, to see a listing of files on drive A:, you could either make drive A: active and then type **DIR**, or you could add the drive letter as a parameter with the DIR command, as in **DIR A:**.

CHANGING THE ACTIVE DIRECTORY

Why Change the Active Directory?

On large disks (such as your hard disk), files are arranged into directories to keep them organized. To work with a file, you first make the directory active that contains it. For example, to run Microsoft Word, a word processing program, you would first make the WORD directory active.

Changing the Active Directory

1. Type **CD *directory***, where *directory* is the name of the directory to which you want to change.

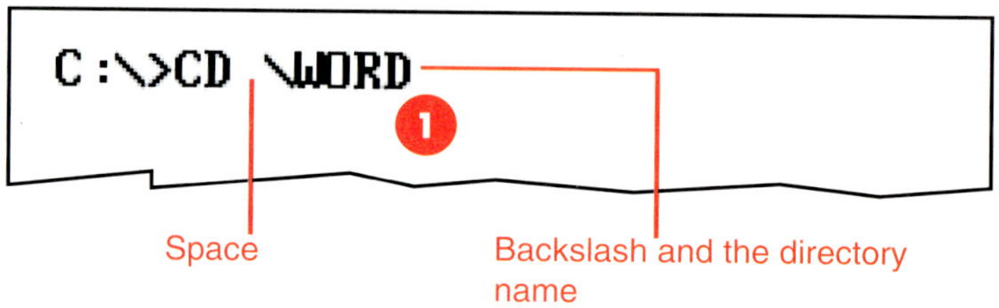

2. Press **Enter**.

TIP

In your startup files, there may be a line that begins with PATH. The PATH statement helps DOS find programs to run, even when their directory is not active. Ask a DOS-wise friend to help set up a PATH statement for you.

TIP

You can work with files in other directories besides the active directory, but you must specify the directory name as a parameter. For example, to see a listing of files in the DOS directory, you could either make the DOS directory active and then type **DIR**, or you could add the directory name as a parameter with the DIR command, as in **DIR \DOS**.

Exercise

This exercise gives you practice changing the active directory. Before trying this exercise, type **C:**, and press **Enter** to make sure C: is your active drive.

1. Type **CD \DOS**.
2. Press **Enter**. The DOS prompt should now show **C:\DOS>**.

TIP

As you saw in the diagram at the beginning of this section, sometimes directories are nested within other directories. If this is the case for the directory to which you want to change, you need to type the complete path in step 1. For example, if you want to change to C:\WORD\SALES, you would type **\WORD\SALES** in step 1.

LEARNING THE LINGO

Root directory: The top directory on the Directory Tree. Because it doesn't have a directory name, such as DOS or WORD, it is indicated by a plain backslash, as in **C:**\.

TIP

When you're finished working with a directory, you should change back to the root directory, the equivalent of the "main lobby" of your disk. Type **CD** \ and press **Enter** to change to the root directory.

LISTING FILES IN THE ACTIVE DIRECTORY

Why List Files in the Active Directory?

If you have several files in a directory, you probably do not remember all their names. Luckily, you don't have to; with a simple DOS command, you can display all the names on the screen.

Listing Files in the Active Directory

1. Change to the directory for which you want to see files.

2. Type **DIR**.

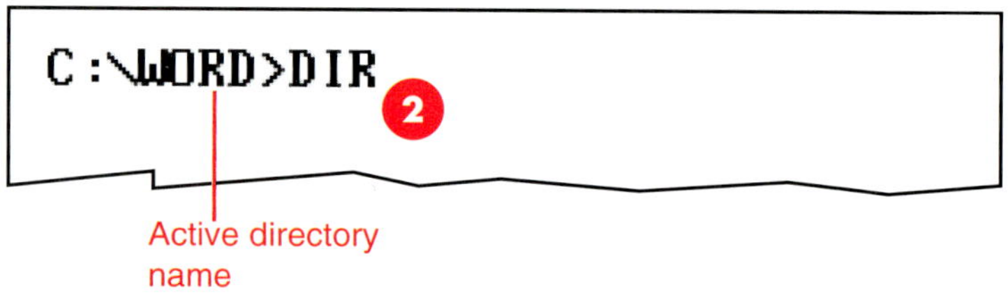

3. Press **Enter**.

QUICK REFRESHER

To change to a directory, type **CD** \ and the directory name. For example, type **CD \WORD** to change to the WORD directory.

TIP

If there are many files in the directory, the names may scroll by too fast. You can remedy this by adding a /W or /P switch to the end of the command, for example, DIR /W or DIR /P. The /W switch displays the files in a wide display, and the /P switch shows the files one page at a time.

LISTING FILES IN A DIFFERENT DIRECTORY

Why List Files in a Different Directory?

Sometimes, you may want to see the contents of a directory other than the active one, but you don't want to bother with the CD (change directory) command. Once again, DOS has anticipated your needs. Instead of changing to the directory, you can simply specify its name in a parameter.

Listing Files in a Different Directory

1. Type **DIR *drive*:*directory***, where *drive* and *directory* are the drive and directory for which you want to display the contents.

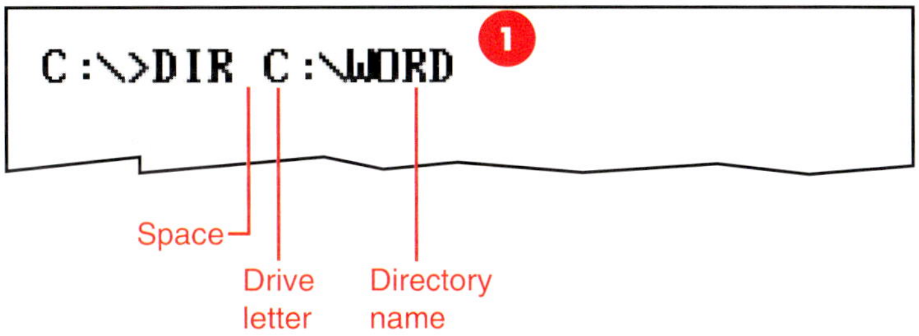

2. Press **Enter**.

QUICK REFRESHER

Remember, a parameter is an extra instruction that lets you tell DOS which disks, files, or directories upon which to act.

TIP

For example, to see a listing of the files on drive A:, you would type **DIR A:**. To see a listing of the files in the TEMP directory of drive D:, you would type **DIR D:\TEMP**.

Working at the DOS Prompt

LISTING ONLY CERTAIN FILES

Why List Only Certain Files?

If there are many files in a directory, you may want to limit the list you see to files with certain names or certain extensions.

To limit the list, you use wild card characters, either an asterisk (*) or a question mark (?). An asterisk represents any combination of characters, while a question mark represents a single character. When you specify files with these wild cards, it's called a *file specification*. Here are some examples:

File Specification	Translation
*.DOC	Files with any name and a DOC extension.
???.DOC	Files with any three-letter name and a DOC extension.
B*.DOC	Files that begin with B and have a DOC extension.
B??.DOC	Files that begin with B and have two other letters in their name, plus a DOC extension.
B*.*	Files that begin with B and have any extension.
B*.???	Files that begin with B and have a three-letter extension.
??CHAP.DOC	Files with any two characters plus CHAP as their name and a DOC extension.

QUICK REFRESHER

Remember, an extension is the file's "last name," the part of its name that appears after the period. The extension often offers clues as to what kind of file it is—files with EXE extensions are usually programs, for example.

Listing Only Certain Files

1. Type **DIR** ***filespec*** where *file-spec* is a file specification.

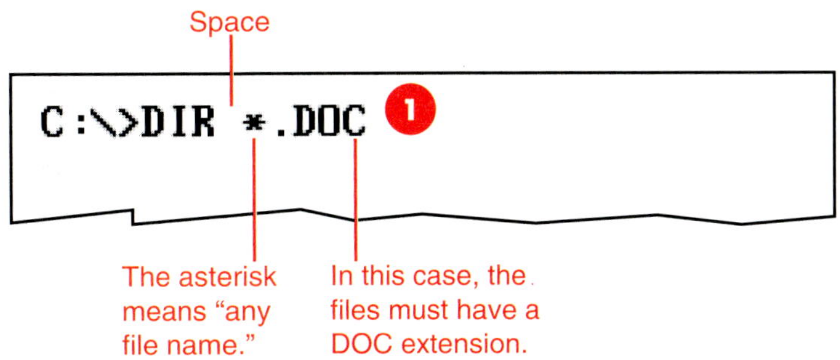

2. Press **Enter**.

LEARNING THE LINGO

Wild card character: A character that stands for any other character. A question mark (?) stands for a single character; an asterisk (*) stands for any number of characters. For example, *.DOC means "a file with any name, of any length, as long as it has an extension of DOC. Here's another: ???.* means "a file with a three-letter name, and any extension of any length.

File specification: When you use wild card characters to specify which files you want a command to act upon, you create a file specification. For example, *.DOC is a file specification. BACKUP.DOC is not a file specification because it contains no * or ?; it's just a file name.

SORTING A FILE LISTING

Why Sort a File Listing?

When you display files with DIR, the files are not shown in any useful order; they're just thrown up on the screen. To sort them logically, you can use the /O switch. Here are a few common uses.

Switch	Sorts Files By
/ON	Name, A to Z
/OE	Extension, A to Z
/OG	Directories first, then files
/OD	Date and time, earliest first
/OS	Size, smallest first

Sorting a File Listing

1. Type **DIR /O** and then one of the letters from the table shown above.

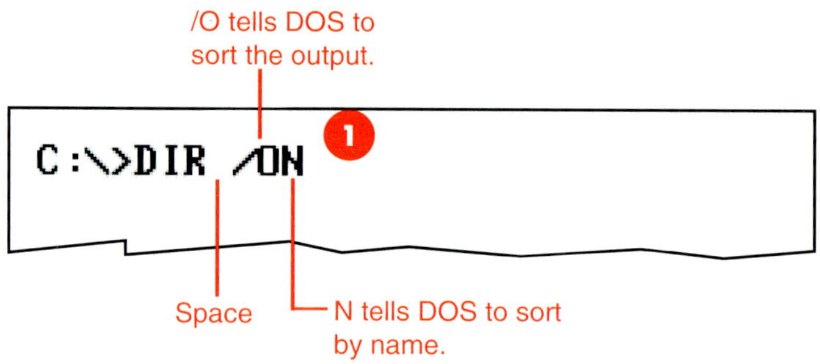

2. Press **Enter**.

Exercise

Ready for a file listing challenge? In this exercise, we'll list all the files from the DOS directory that end in .EXE, one page at a time, by size from largest to smallest. This will give you a chance to practice several of the DIR-based skills you have learned.

1. Type **DIR C:\DOS*.EXE /O-S /P**.

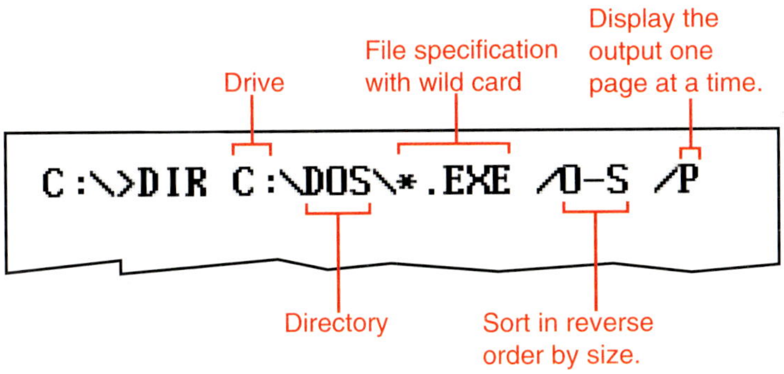

2. Press **Enter**.

TIP

To reverse the order, place a minus sign between the O and the second letter. For example, **DIR /O-N** would show files in reverse alphabetical order, Z to A.

CREATING A DIRECTORY

Why Create a Directory?

Some directories come pre-installed on your computer, such as DOS. Other directories are created by installation programs when you install new software, such as Windows and Word. But sometimes, you may want to create a directory to keep data files separate, or you may want a new directory to store a program that does not come with an installation utility.

Directory names can be up to eight characters long and have a three-character extension, just like file names can. However, most people don't use extensions for directory names. Directory names without extensions are much easier to distinguish from file names.

Creating a Directory

1. Type **MD *directory*** where *directory* is the directory name to create.

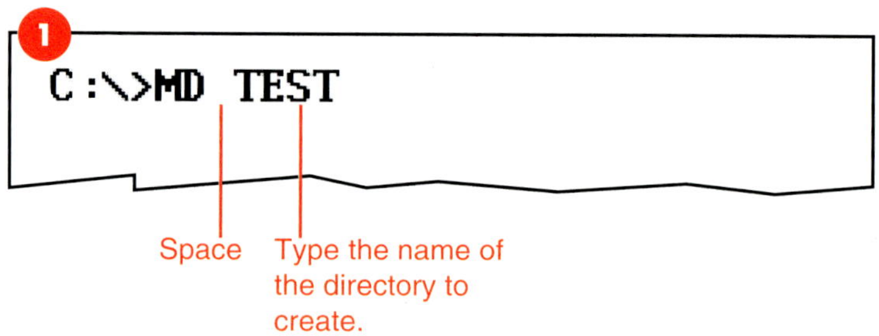

2. Press **Enter**.

TIP

Before creating a new directory, change to the root directory by typing **CD ** and pressing **Enter**. Or if you want the new directory to be a subdirectory of an existing directory, change to the existing directory—for example, **CD \WORD**.

Exercise

In this exercise, we'll create a directory off the root directory called PRACTICE.

1. Change to the root directory (type **CD** \ and press **Enter**).
2. Type MD PRACTICE.

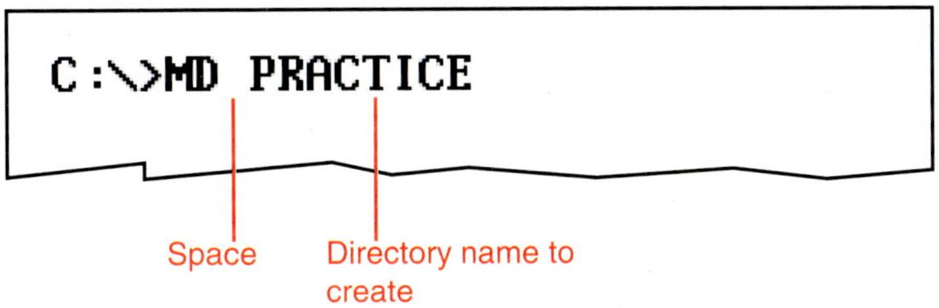

3. Press **Enter**.

QUICK REFRESHER

To change to the root directory, type **CD** \ and press **Enter**.

DELETING A DIRECTORY

Why Delete a Directory?

You delete a directory when it has outlived its usefulness. For example, if you created a directory for 1991 taxes called 1991TAX, and then deleted all the files from it when they became obsolete, you might want to get rid of the 1991TAX directory to keep your hard disk tidy.

There are two ways to delete directories. The RD (remove directory) command requires that a directory be empty and have no subdirectories under it. The DELTREE command has no such requirements; it wipes out not only the directory, but any files and subdirectories left within it.

Deleting a Directory with the RD Command

1. Change to the directory immediately above the directory you want to delete.

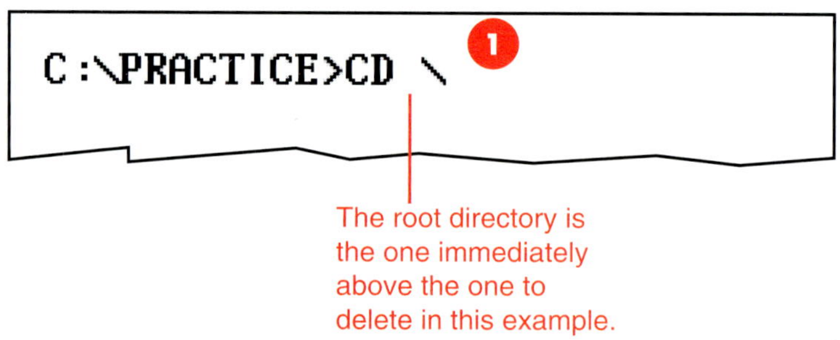

2. Type **RD *directory*** where *directory* is the name of the directory to delete.

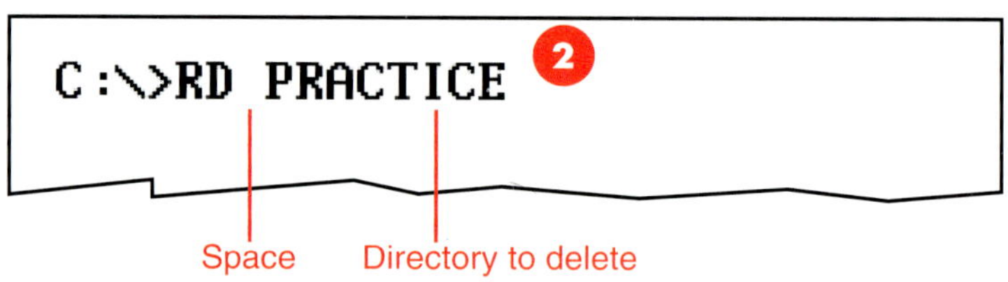

3. Press **Enter**.

TIP

The RD command will not work unless the directory is completely empty. If the directory is not empty, use DELTREE instead.

Deleting a Directory with the DELTREE Command

1. Change to the directory immediately above the directory you want to delete.

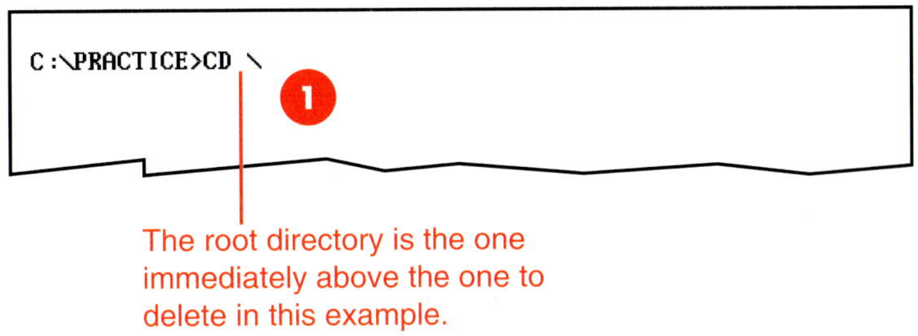

2. Type **DELTREE *directory*** where *directory* is the name of the directory to delete.

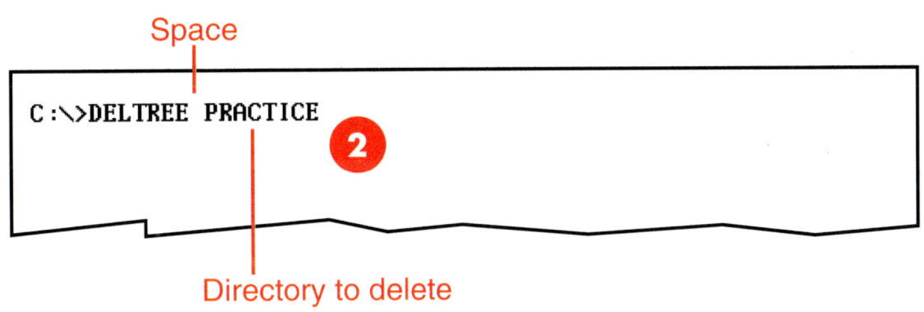

3. Press Enter.

4. Type **Y** to confirm.

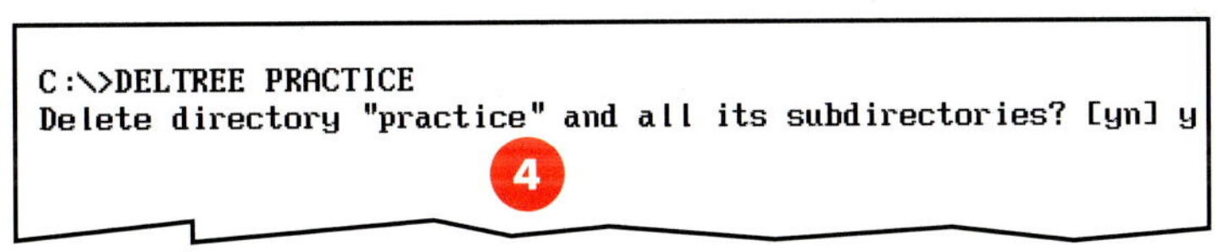

5. Press **Enter**.

TIP

For example, in step 1, if you want to delete C:\PRACTICE, change to the root directory by typing **CD **. If you want to delete SALES in C:\WORD\SALES, change to WORD by typing **CD \WORD**.

COPYING A FILE

Why Copy A File?

People copy files because they realize that accidents can happen. For example, you might copy an accounting file onto a floppy disk and store the floppy disk in a different building, so in the event of a disaster, the files would be safe. On a much less grand scale, you might simply want to make a copy of a file before you change it, so you'll be able to retain the original.

When you copy a file, unless the file is in the active directory, you must tell DOS where the file currently resides. Along these same lines, unless the copy is going to go in the active directory, you must specify a destination for the copy.

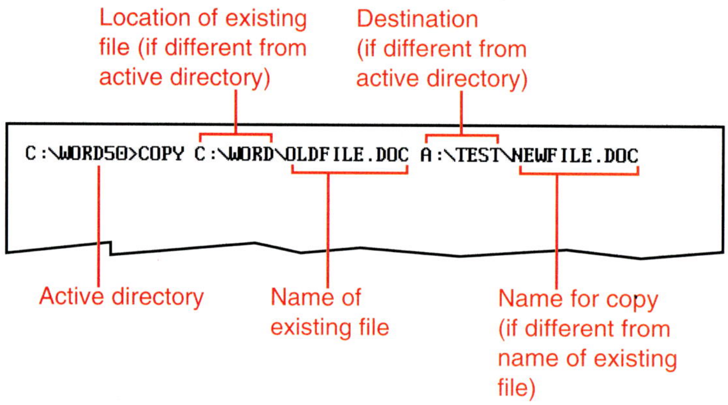

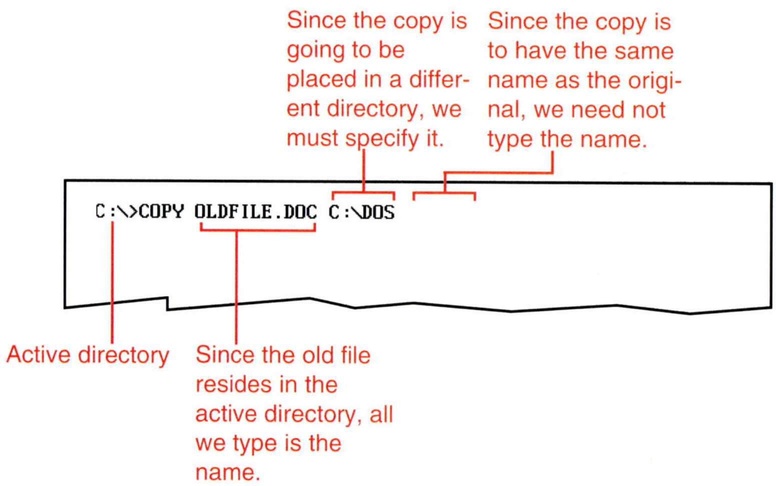

Copying a Single File

1. Type **COPY *oldfile.ext newfile.ext***, specifying the locations if they differ from the active directory. Type the existing file name for *oldfile.ext* and the desired name for the copy for *newfile.ext*.

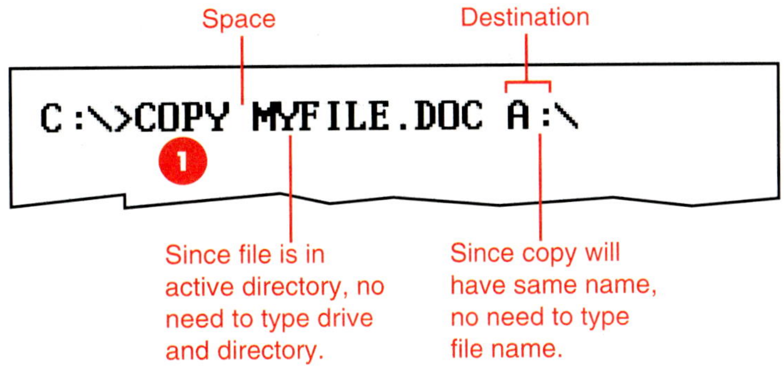

2. Press **Enter**.

TIP

The copy of the file need not have the same name as the original. In fact, if the copy is to be located in the same directory as the original, it *cannot* have the same name, because you cannot have two files with the same name in the same directory.

COPYING SEVERAL FILES

Why Copy Several Files?

After you've used the procedure for copying a single file several times, you may wonder "isn't there a way to do several files at once?" The answer is yes, as long as the files have something in common.

> **QUICK REFRESHER**
>
> Remember, an asterisk (*) stands for any group of characters; for example, *.DOC means any file name as long as it has an extension of DOC. A question mark (?) means any single character. For example, ???.DOC means any file name as long as the name is three letters long and has an extension of DOC.

To copy several files at once, you must use wild card characters to create a file specification.

```
C:\>COPY C:\DOS\*.SYS A:\
```

Asterisk means "any file name."

```
C:\>COPY CHAP??.PCX C:\DOS\CHAP??.BAK
```

CHAP?? means "any file that consists of CHAP plus two characters at the end."

Notice that you can specify a different extension for the copies.

```
C:\>COPY *.??K B:\
```

This file specification means "any name, and a three-character extension, the last character of which must be K."

Copying Several Files

1. Type **COPY** and then a file specification that describes the group of files you want to copy. Then type the drive and directory where you want the files to be copied.

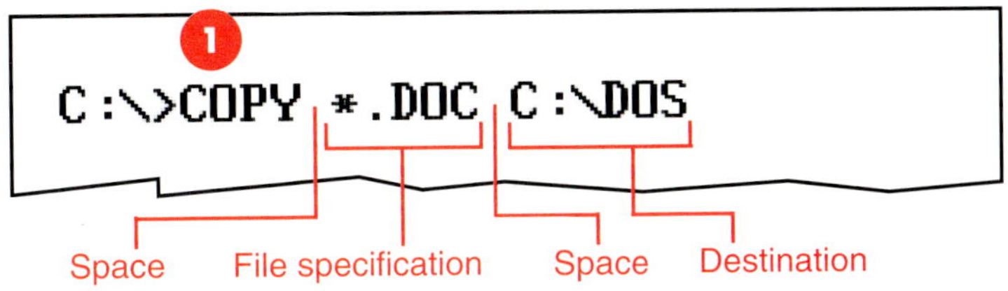

2. Press **Enter**.

Exercise

In this exercise, you'll create a directory, as you learned to do in the "Creating a Directory" task. Then you'll copy all the files from the DOS directory that end in .SYS to the new directory, renaming their extensions to .BAK. Finally, you'll use DELTREE to get rid of the whole mess you created.

1. Change to the root directory (type **CD** \, and press **Enter**).

2. Create a directory called TEST (type **MD TEST**, and press **Enter**).

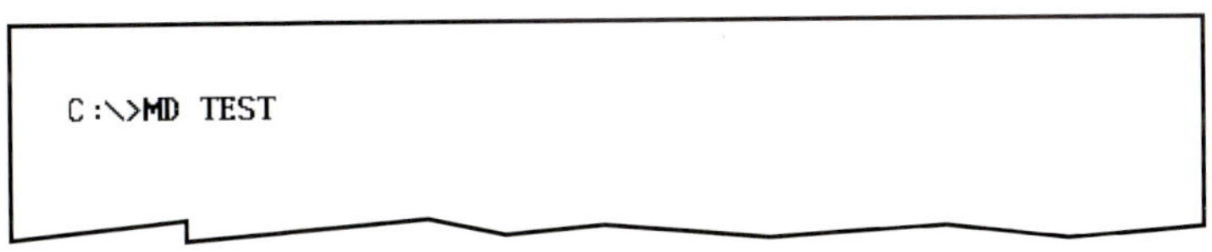

3. Type **COPY C:\DOS*.SYS C:\TEST*.BAK**, and press **Enter**.

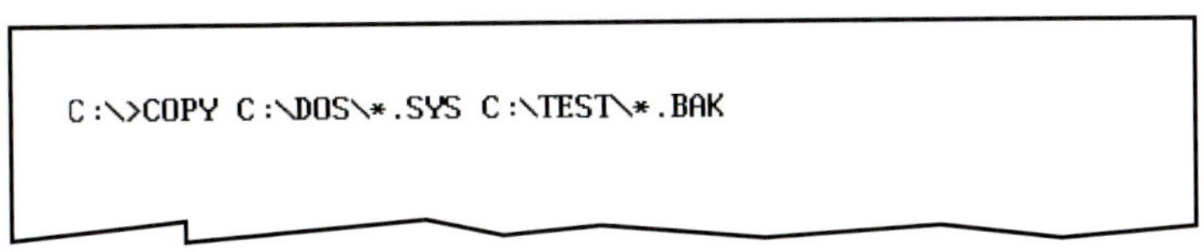

4. Change to the TEST directory (type **CD \TEST**, and press **Enter**).

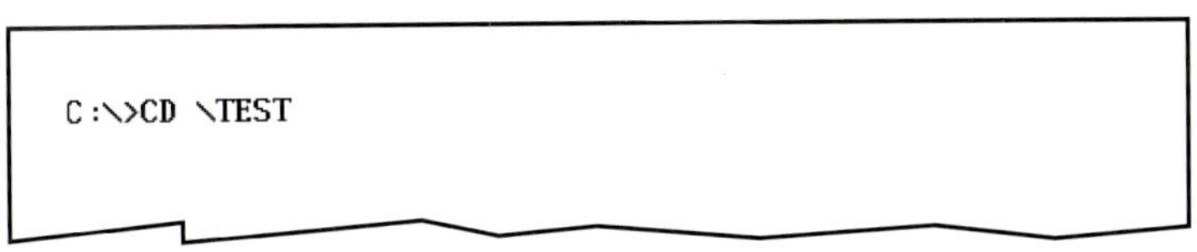

COPYING SEVERAL FILES

5. List the files in the TEST directory to check your work (type **DIR**, and press **Enter**).

```
C:\TEST>DIR
```

6. Change back to the root directory (type **CD** \ and press **Enter**).

```
C:\TEST>CD \
```

7. Remove the TEST directory (type **DELTREE**, and press **Enter**, then answer **Yes**).

```
C:\>DELTREE TEST
Delete directory "test" and all its subdirectories? [yn] y
```

Answer Y when prompted.

MOVING A FILE

Why Move a File?

No matter how carefully you plan when you store a file, eventually you will want it stored somewhere else. You might move an important file into its own directory (see the "Creating a Directory" task) or move a backup file onto a floppy disk for storage.

When you move a file, unless the file is in the active directory, you must tell DOS where the file currently resides. You must also specify the location to which the file should be moved.

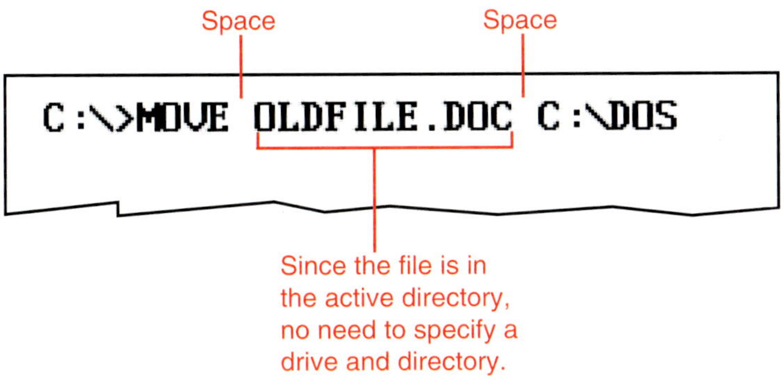

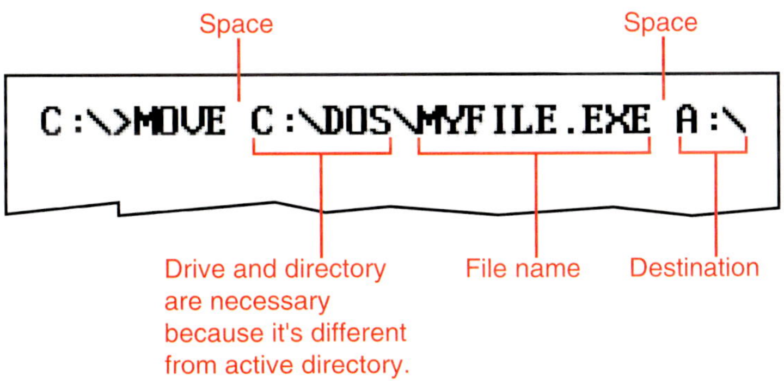

TIP

Moving a file is a lot like copying it and then deleting the old one. In fact, before DOS 6 introduced the MOVE command, copying-then-deleting was the only way DOS users could move files.

Moving a File

1. Type **MOVE** ***filename.ext destination*** where *filename.ext* is the name of the file to move and *destination* is the place to move it.

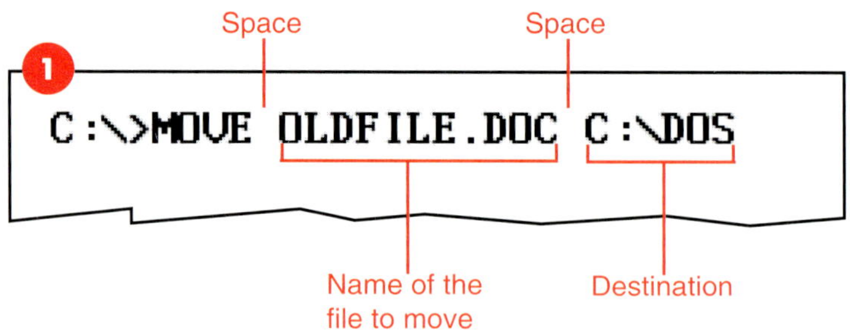

2. Press **Enter**.

TIP

If you want to rename a file as you're moving it, tack on a name after the destination. For example, to rename TEST.DOC to TEST.BAK as you move it from C:\ to C:\DOS, you would type **MOVE C:\TEST.DOC C:\DOS\TEST.BAK**.

Exercise

In this exercise, you'll move a mostly useless DOS command called NLSFUNC.EXE from the DOS directory to the root directory, renaming it as you go. Then you'll move it back and rename it back to its original name.

1. Type **MOVE C:\DOS\NLSFUNC.EXE C:\NLSFUNC.BAK** and press **Enter**.

```
C:\>MOVE C:\DOS\NLSFUNC.EXE C:\NLSFUNC.BAK
```

2. (Optional)Type **DIR C:*.BAK** and press **Enter** to verify that the move was successful.

```
C:\>DIR *.BAK
```

3. Type **MOVE C:\NLSFUNC.BAK C:\DOS\NLSFUNC.EXE** and press **Enter**.

```
C:\>MOVE C:\NLSFUNC.BAK C:\DOS\NLSFUNC.EXE
```

TIP

NLSFUNC.EXE controls foreign language support for your keyboard. If you are using foreign language support, use a different command instead for this exercise. SUBST.EXE is a good choice, or XMA2EMS.SYS.

MOVING SEVERAL FILES

Why Move Several Files?

Moving files one at a time can get tedious. If the files you want to move have something in common—for example, the same extension, the same first three letters, or any other part of their name the same—you can use a file specification to move them.

Moving Several Files

1. Type **MOVE**, then a file specification that describes the group of files you want to move.

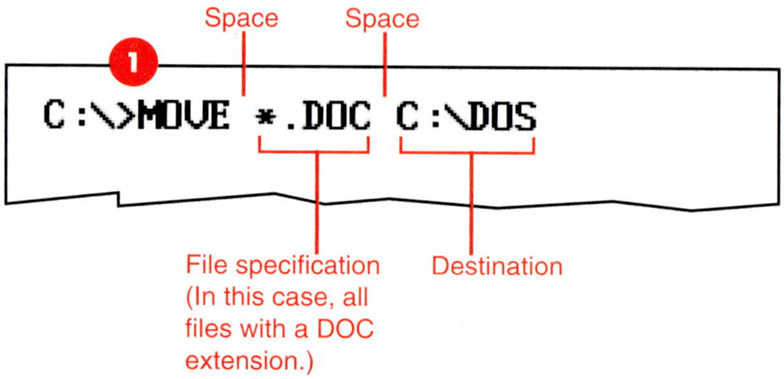

2. Press **Enter**.

QUICK REFRESHER

Here's a brief review of file specifications. An asterisk (*) stands for any group of characters; for example, *.DOC means any file name as long as it has an extension of DOC. A question mark (?) means any single character. For example, ???.DOC means any file name as long as it is three letters and has an extension of DOC. Turn back to the "Listing Only Certain Files" task for more examples.

RENAMING FILES

Why Rename Files?

You might want to rename files for a variety of reasons. For example, if you finish working on a document called TEMP.DOC, you might want to rename it FINAL.DOC. Or if you want to camouflage a personnel file so that someone snooping through your computer will not notice it, you might rename it something mundane like DOGFOOD.LOG.

Renaming a File

1. Type **REN *oldname.ext newname.ext*** where *oldname.ext* is the current file name and *newname.ext* is the name to which you want to rename it.

```
C:\>REN C:\WORD\OLDFILE.DOC NEWFILE.DOC
```

1

2. Press **Enter**.

TIP

If the file is in a different directory than the active one, include the file's location in the command. For example, **REN C:\DOS\TESTFILE.EXE C:\DOS\MYFILE.EXE**.

DELETING FILES

Why Delete a File?

When a file has outlived its usefulness, you can delete it to free up the space on your disk. If your old files contain sensitive information, such as personnel or payroll records, you may want to delete them as a security measure.

Deleting a Single File

1. Change to the directory containing the file. (Type **CD *directory***, where directory is the directory name, and press **Enter.**)

```
C:\>CD \DOS
```

2. Type **DEL *filename.ext*** where *filename.ext* is the name of the file to delete.

```
C:\DOS>DEL TEST.BAK
```

3. Press **Enter**.

TIP

Even though a file has been deleted, it can sometimes be recovered with the Undelete command. See the "Undeleting Files" task later in this section.

QUICK REFRESHER

Remember, *wild cards* are asterisks or question marks. Asterisks represent any number of characters, while question marks represent single characters. When you specify a group of files with a wild card, it's called a *file specification*.

Deleting Several Files At Once

To delete multiple files, you must use wild cards to create file specifications. See the "Listing Only Certain Files" task for complete details.

1. Change to the directory where the files are located.

2. Type **DEL** ***filespec*** where *filespec* is the file specification describing the files to be deleted.

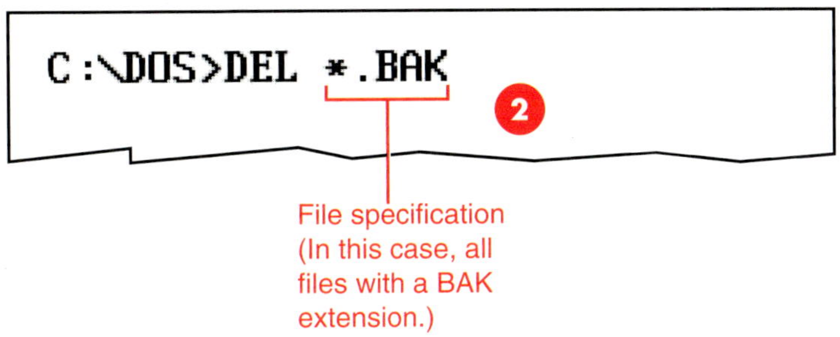

3. Press **Enter**.

TIP

If you type ***.*** in step 2 to delete all the files in the directory, DOS will ask you to confirm the deletion. If asked, type **Y** for Yes.

SETTING UP DELETE PROTECTION

Why Set Up Delete Protection?

DOS has a handy Undelete command that you'll learn about in the next task. It allows you to bring files back to life that have been deleted. However, used by itself, the Undelete command is limited. If you use it immediately after the deletion, your chances of recovering the file are very good, but the longer you wait and the more operations you perform afterwards, the slimmer your hopes of recovery.

DOS provides two methods of improving your undeletion chances: Delete Tracker and Delete Sentry. You should set up one now to prepare for future disasters.

- **Delete Tracker** increases your chances of successfully recovering a deleted file. It takes up some of your computer's memory, so you may not want to use Delete Tracker if your computer is short on memory.
- **Delete Sentry** offers the highest level of file deletion protection, but requires some of your hard disk space. If you are already short on hard disk space, consider using Delete Tracker instead.

Setting Up Delete Tracker

1. Type **UNDELETE /T** followed by your hard drive's letter (for example, C). Type a minus sign (-), and then the maximum number of deleted files that you want DOS to keep track of—for example, -50.

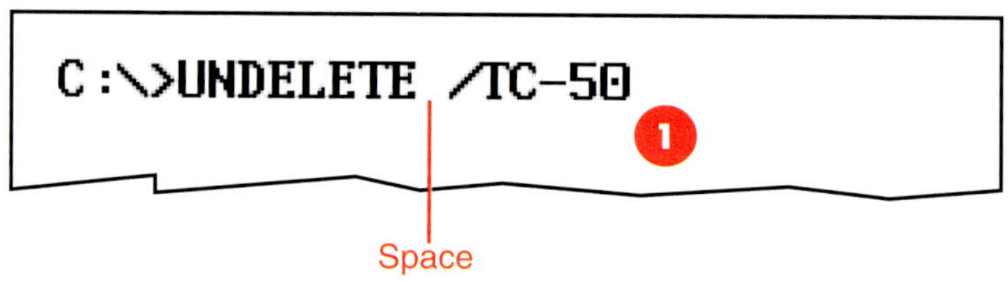

2. Press **Enter**.

TIP

The higher the number you use in step 2, the more of your computer's memory will be used up.

TIP

You can start Delete Tracker or Delete Sentry each time you turn on your computer by following the steps in this book, but it may be easier to add the command to your startup file. Ask a computer-savvy friend to help.

Setting Up Delete Sentry

1. Type **UNDELETE /S** and then your hard drive's letter (for example, C).

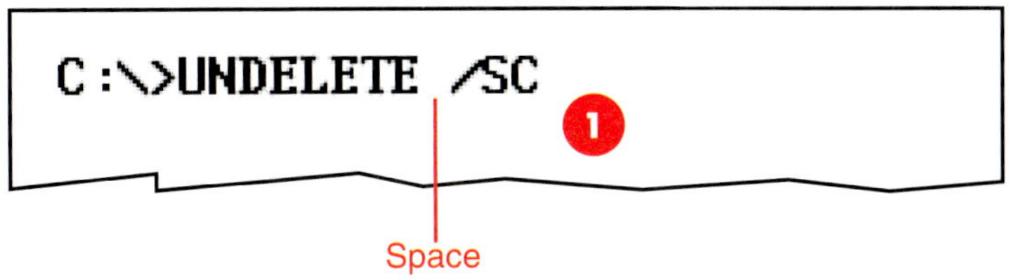

2. Press **Enter**.

TIP

If you load Delete Tracker or Delete Sentry and then realize that it is using up more of your system resources than you can spare, you can either restart your computer or stop Delete Tracker or Delete Sentry from running. Just type **UNDELETE /UNLOAD**.

UNDELETING FILES

Why Undelete Files?

Accidents happen, and sometimes you delete a file that you didn't mean to. Or you delete a file and then later realize that the file was valuable. DOS has you covered with the Undelete command.

Undeleting a Single File

1. Change to the directory where the deleted file used to reside.

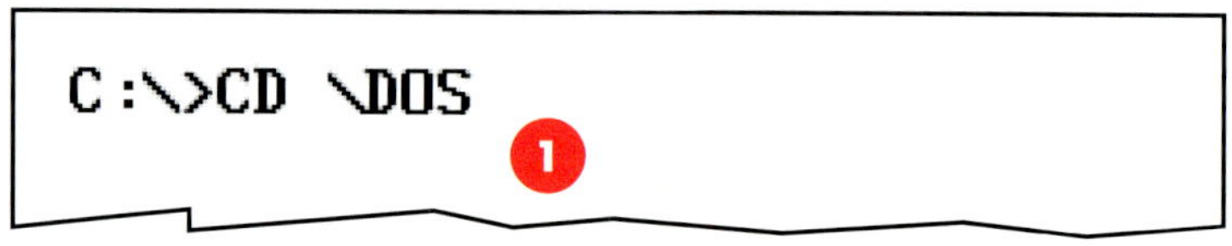

2. Type **UNDELETE *filename.ext*** where *filename.ext* is the name of the file to be undeleted.

3. Type / and then the code for the delete protection method you are using.

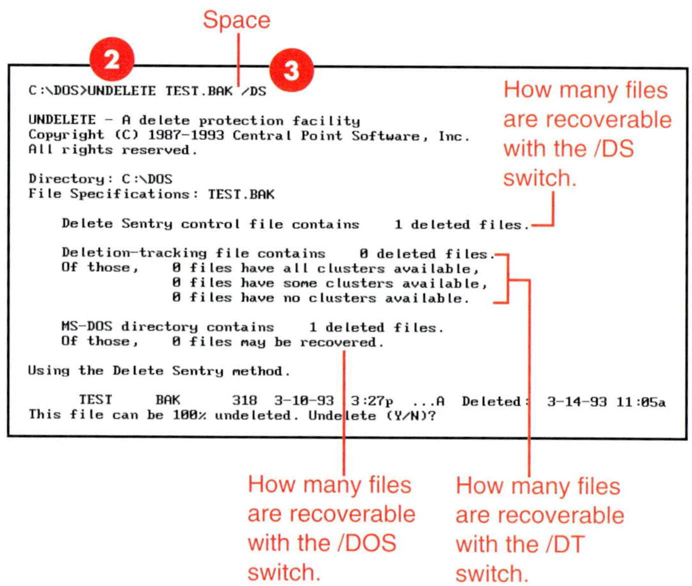

4. Press **Enter**.

5. Answer **Yes** when asked to confirm.

Undeleting Several Files

1. Change to the directory where the deleted files used to reside.

```
C:\>CD \DOS
```

2. Type **UNDELETE** / and then the code for the delete protection method you are using.

```
C:\DOS>UNDELETE /DOS
```

3. Press **Enter**.

ENTER

4. For each file that appears, answer **Y** to undelete it or **N** to skip it.
5. If prompted, type the first letter of the deleted file's name.
6. Repeat steps 4 and 5, as needed.

```
    Delete Sentry control file contains    1 deleted files.

    Deletion-tracking file contains    0 deleted files.
    Of those,    0 files have all clusters available,
                 0 files have some clusters available,
                 0 files have no clusters available.

    MS-DOS directory contains    4 deleted files.
    Of those,    4 files may be recovered.

Using the MS-DOS directory method.

      ?PBACKUP BAT       22  6-19-92  1:24p  ....  Undelete (Y/N)?y
      Please type the first character for ?PBACKU.BAT: C

File successfully undeleted.

      ?NSET    BAT       24  5-14-92  9:39a  ....  Undelete (Y/N)?y
      Please type the first character for ?NSET   .BAT: I

File successfully undeleted.

      ?        BAT        6  7-22-92 10:44a  ....  Undelete (Y/N)?y
      Please type the first character for ?       .BAT:
```

TIP

When you undelete a file, you should specify a code to tell DOS which delete protection method you are using:

/DT	for Delete Tracker
/DS	for Delete Sentry
/DOS	for neither

DOS can "play dumb" with you and pretend that a file can't be recovered if you don't specify the protection method that was enabled when the file was deleted. If you're sure a file should be recoverable but it's not working, try again using a different code.

FORMATTING A DISK

Why Format a Disk?

When you buy diskettes (floppy disks), unless the box says "preformatted for IBM," you must format each diskette before you use it. Formatting lays down a "grid" on which DOS can write data; think of it as putting lines on a sheet of notebook paper before you write on it. You can reformat a disk that is already formatted, but **formatting destroys any information that is already on a diskette**, so you must be sure that a used disk contains no valuable data before you format it.

Formatting a Diskette

1. Insert the diskette to be formatted in drive A: or B:.
2. Type **FORMAT *letter*** where *letter* is the drive letter containing the diskette (A: or B:).
3. Press **Enter**.
4. When asked to press **Enter** when ready, do so.
5. Wait for DOS to finish formatting.
6. When prompted, type a label (disk name) if you want.
7. Press **Enter**.
8. Type **N** for No when asked if you want to format another.
9. Press **Enter**.

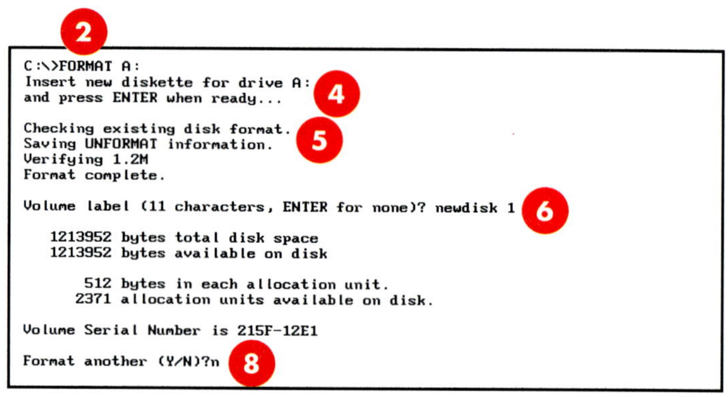

TIP

In the next section, you'll learn about transferring system files to a diskette to make it bootable (able to be used to start up the computer). You can make a diskette bootable as you are formatting it by adding the /S switch to the formatting command—for example, **FORMAT A: /S**.

TIP

There are two sizes of floppy disk drives: 5 1/4-inch and 3 1/2-inch. For each size, there are two disk densities: double and high. If you bought your computer within the last three years, it probably has high-density drives. Check your owner's manual if you're not sure.

Although a high-density drive can read either double- or high-density diskettes, you should stick to the same diskette type as your drive for best results.

CREATING A SYSTEM DISKETTE

What Is a System Diskette?

A system diskette is a diskette that contains the special, hidden files that DOS needs to boot (start) itself. These files are normally hidden on your hard drive, so that when you turn the power on, the computer starts.

As a safety precaution, in case something happens to your hard disk, you may want to create a system diskette. You can start your computer from the system diskette if you have to, by placing the system diskette in your drive A: before you turn on the power.

Creating a System Diskette

1. Place a blank, formatted floppy disk in drive A:.
2. Type **SYS A:**.
3. Press **Enter**.
4. Wait for the message **System Transferred** to appear.

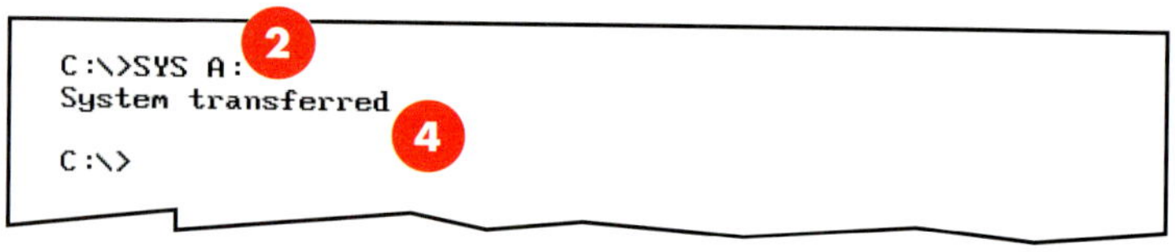

TIP

You may also want to copy two files from your hard disk to your system diskette: AUTOEXEC.BAT and CONFIG.SYS. These are startup files that tell your computer exactly how you prefer for it to operate. If these two files are on your system diskette, your system will run much more normally when started from the system diskette than if they weren't there. See the "Copying Files" task to learn how to copy them there.

LEARNING THE LINGO

System diskette: A diskette that contains IO.SYS, MSDOS.SYS, and COMMAND.COM, the three files that DOS needs to start itself. Of these, the first two are hidden, so you won't see them when you use DIR to see the disk contents.

Boot: To start up a computer. The term comes from "pull up by the bootstraps."

TIP

In step 1, you must use drive A, not drive B. When your computer starts up, it checks drive A: to see if there is a diskette in it. If there is, that diskette takes precedence over the hard disk, and DOS boots from the diskette. DOS does not check drive B at all during this process.

PART 3

Handy DOS 6 Utilities

Before DOS 6, users often made up for DOS's shortcomings by buying extra utility programs. These programs helped make backups, cleaned up disk clutter, checked for computer viruses, and more.

DOS 6 is different from previous DOS versions, however—it comes with some very useful utility programs that you can use without buying anything extra. In this section, you'll learn how to take advantage of these neat extras.

The steps in this section move at a quicker pace with a bit less explanation than the previous two sections. If you have trouble keeping up, or are getting lost in the menus and boxes, review Part I to learn some basics before tackling the utilities.

BACKING UP YOUR HARD DISK

Why Back Up Your Hard Disk?

You back up your hard disk for the same reason that you buy auto insurance—because sooner or later an accident will happen. And even though it won't necessarily be your fault, you're the one who will have to fix it.

In the case of your hard disk, that accident could be any of several catastrophes. Your entire hard disk could have a mechanical breakdown or experience complete amnesia one morning. You could accidentally reformat your hard disk, wiping out all its data. You could accidentally delete all the files in your root directory. I could go on, but you've probably got the message by now. Back up your hard disk. Do it *now*.

QUICK REFRESHER

As you may remember from working with the DOS Shell, to select something, double-click on it with the mouse, or **Tab** to it and press **Enter**.

TIP

DOS 6 comes with a Windows-based version of MS Backup. When you installed DOS, you chose whether or not you wanted the Windows version installed. The Windows version operates almost identically to the non-Windows version shown here.

Backing Up Your Entire Hard Disk

1. Type **MSBACKUP** at the DOS prompt, and press **Enter** to start MS Backup.

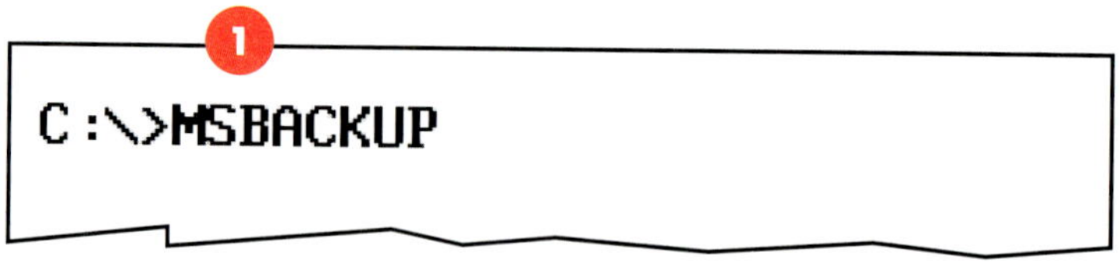

2. If you get the message **Backup requires configuration for this computer**, skip to the "Configuring MS Backup for Your Computer" task, then return to this procedure when you're finished.

If you get this message, skip to the "Configuring MS Backup for Your Computer" task, then return to this procedure.

3. Select **B**ackup, or press **Enter**.

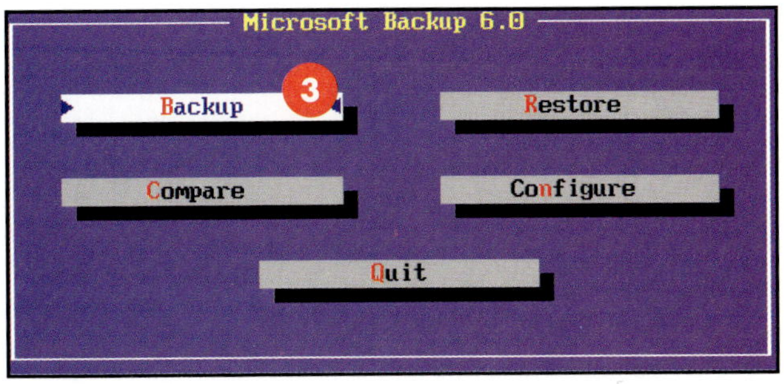

4. Check how many disks you will need, and locate them so they'll be handy.

5. Choose **S**tart Backup.

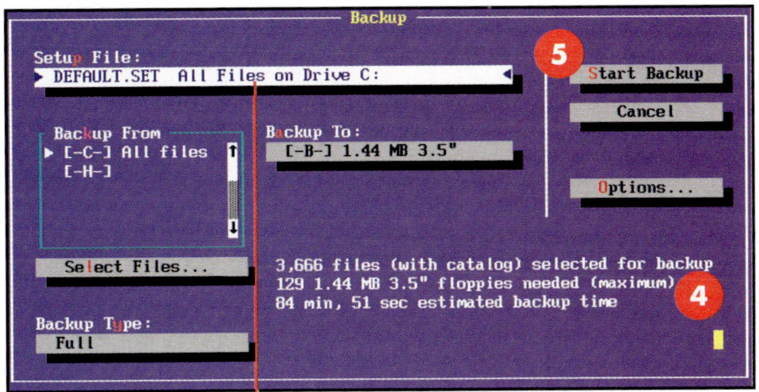

You can change the destination by selecting this box.

6. When prompted, insert the first diskette in the drive, and choose **C**ontinue or press **Enter**.

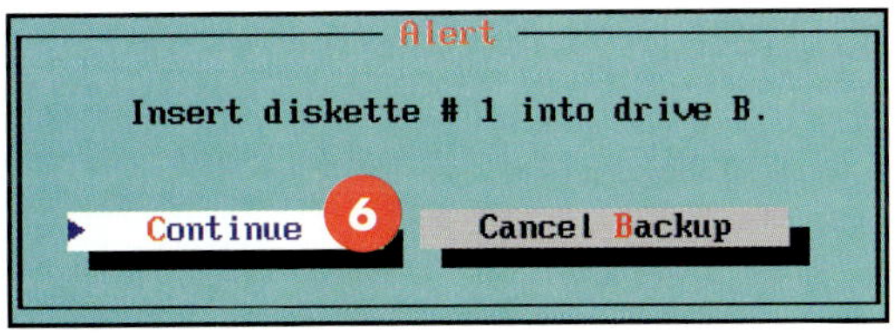

TIP

You can back up only certain files on your hard disk if you want to, but that procedure is beyond the scope of this book. Refer to your DOS manual for details.

TIP

If you're not happy with the type of diskettes that MS Backup has specified, select B**a**ckup To and select a different disk type before performing step 5.

BACKING UP YOUR HARD DISK

7. When prompted, insert the next diskette in the drive.

8. Continue inserting diskettes when prompted until the back-up is complete.

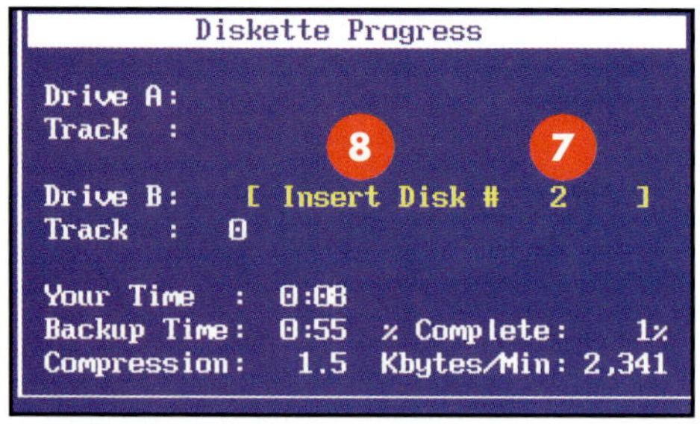

9. Press **Enter** or select **OK** at the Backup Complete box.

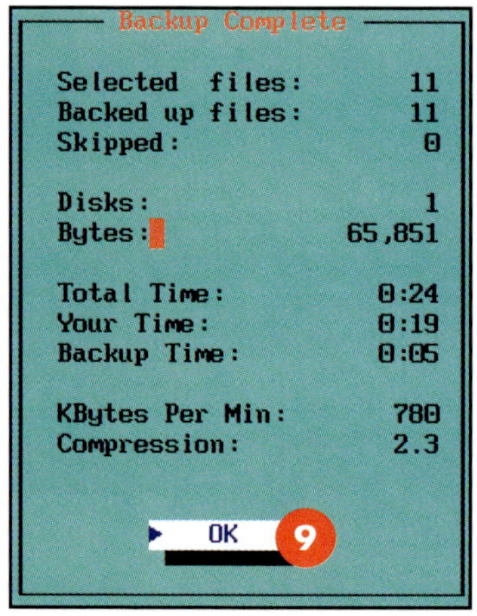

10. Select **Quit** to exit MS Backup.

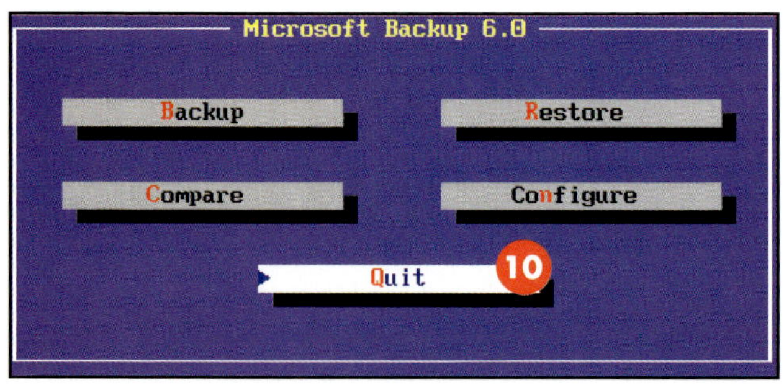

LEARNING THE LINGO

Backup catalog: A file that contains an index of all the files backed up. MS Backup uses the backup catalog when it restores the files (see the Restoring Files to your Hard Disk task).

TIP

Label each disk with the date, the backup catalog number (the thing that ends in .FUL on the screen), and the disk number. For example, the first disk is disk 1, and so on.

CONFIGURING MS BACKUP FOR YOUR COMPUTER

Why Configure MS Backup?

Because all computers are different, MS Backup includes a configuration program that starts automatically the first time you run the program. This configuration program checks your floppy disk drives and performs a small sample backup to make sure your drives will back up files reliably.

The following procedure assumes that you tried to start MSBACKUP and were told that **Backup Requires Configuration for This Computer**. If you got that message, you're in the right place—just follow these steps.

QUICK REFRESHER

As you may remember from working with the DOS Shell, to select something, double-click on it with the mouse, or **Tab** to it, and press **Enter**.

LEARNING THE LINGO

Configuration: The process of setting up a program to work with your particular model of computer and to work according to your preferences.

Configuring MS Backup

1. Select **S**tart Configuration.

2. Wait for MS Backup to pause at the Video and Mouse Configuration screen, then select **OK**, or press **Enter** to continue.

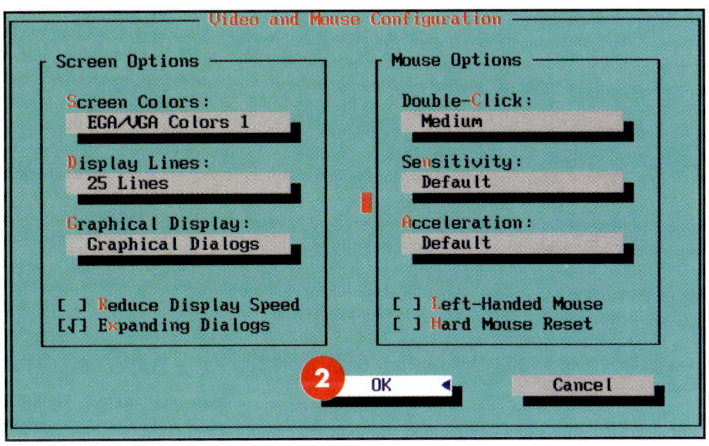

CONFIGURING MS BACKUP FOR YOUR COMPUTER

3 Wait for the Floppy Drive Change Line Test window to appear, then select **Start Test**, or press **Enter**.

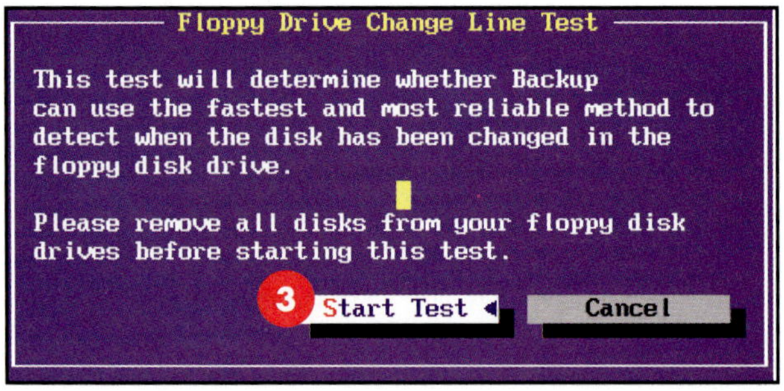

4 At the Backup Devices window, select **OK**, or press **Enter** to continue.

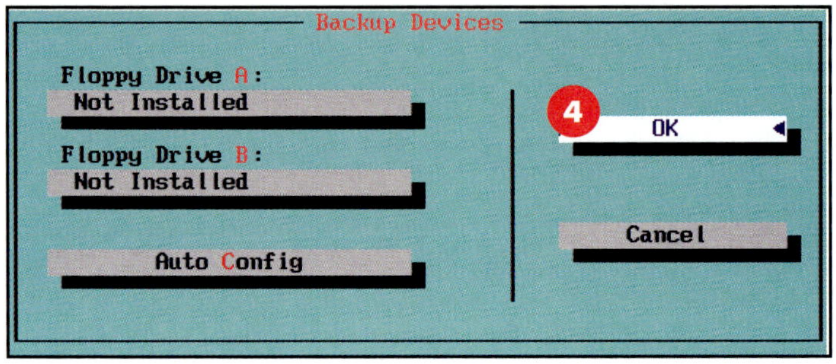

5 Wait for the Processor Speed Test and Hard Disk Read Test to finish and the Performance Index to briefly display.

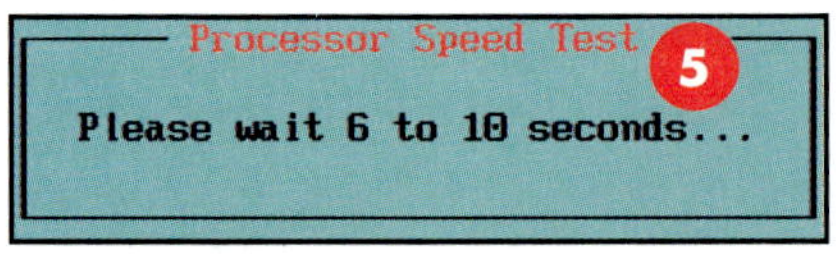

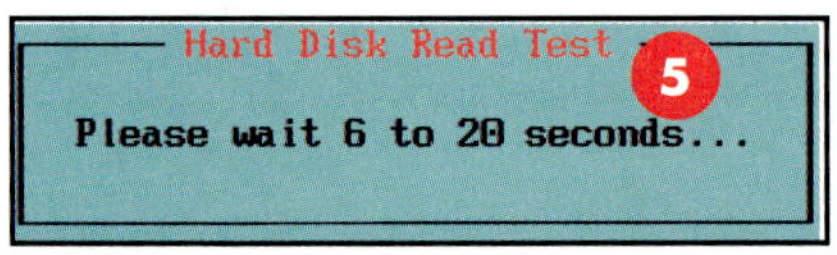

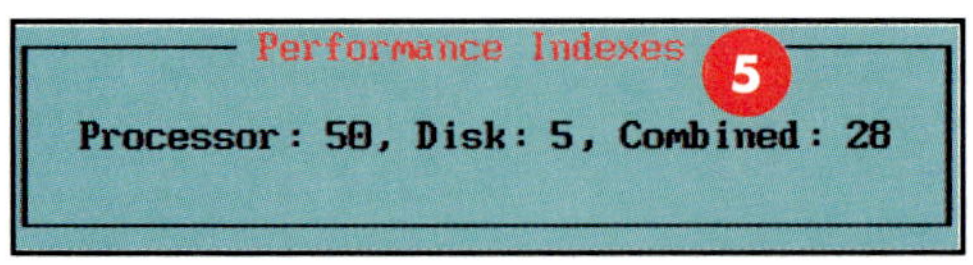

6. At the Floppy Disk Compatibility Test box, select **Start Test**, or press **Enter**.

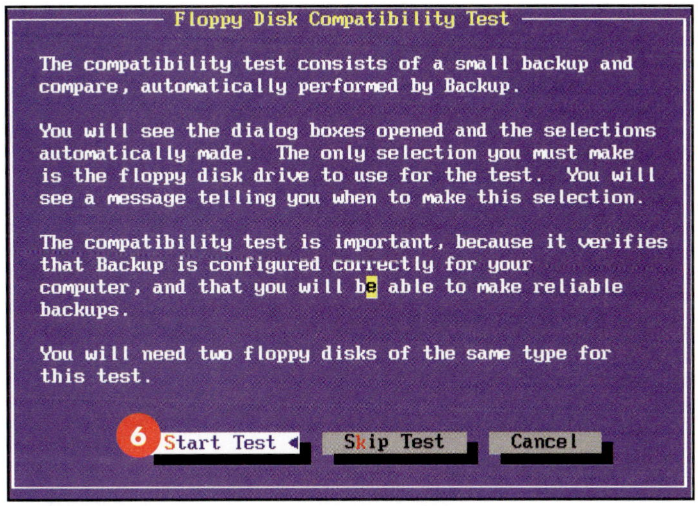

7. At the Alert box, select **Continue**, or press **Enter**.

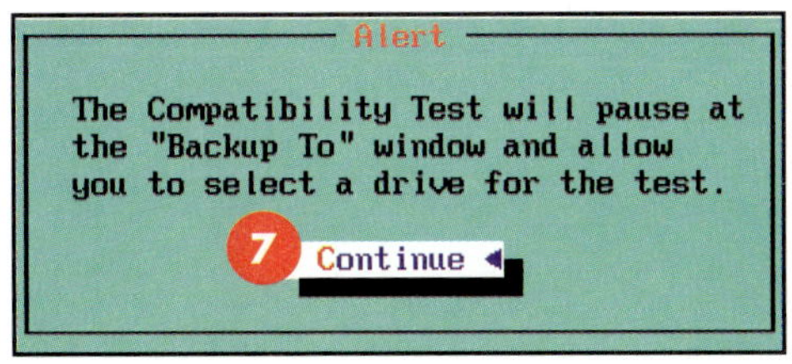

8. At the Backup To box, click on the disk type you want to use for the test, or **Tab** to the desired type, and press the **Spacebar**.

9. Select **OK**, or press **Enter** when the correct disk type is selected.

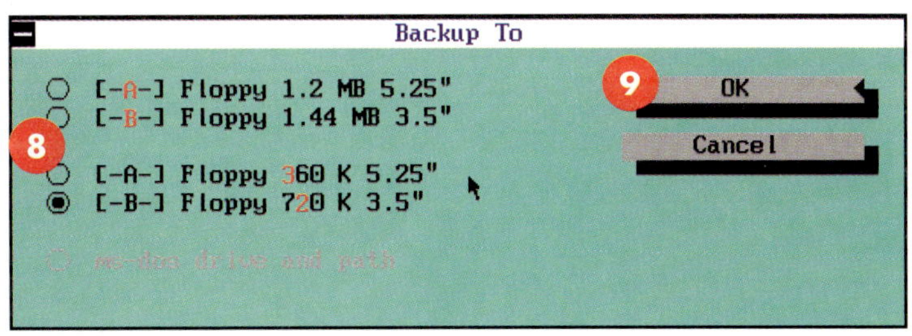

10. Wait until you're asked to insert Disk 1 into the drive, then do so.

11. Select Continue, or press **Enter**.

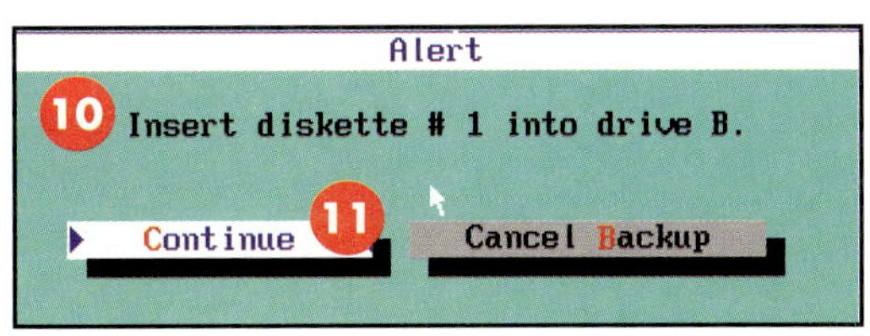

12 If you get a message that the disk contains files, choose **Overwrite** to continue.

13 Wait until the message to Insert Disk #2 appears, then do so.

14 If you get a message that the disk contains files, choose **Overwrite** to continue.

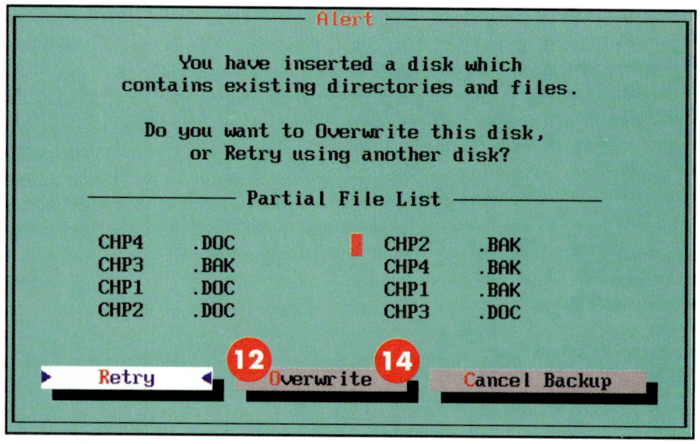

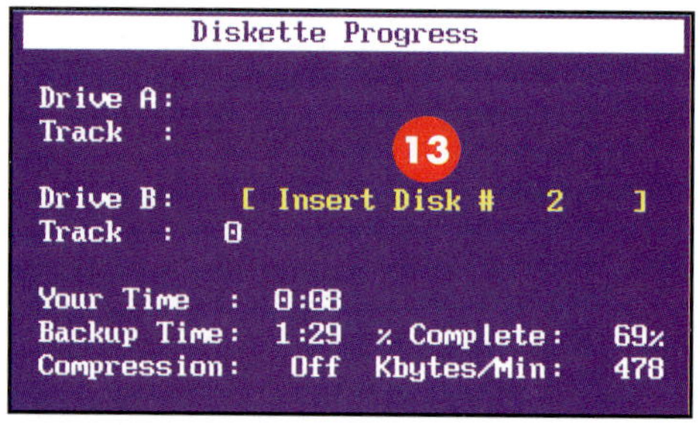

15 Wait for the Backup Complete window to appear, then select **OK**, or press **Enter**.

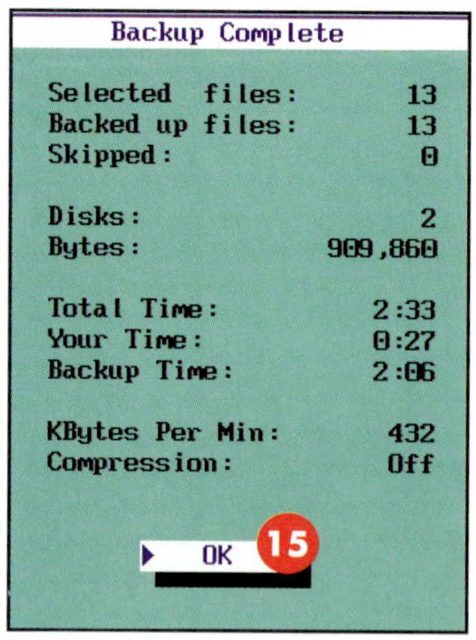

16 Wait until you're told to insert diskette #1, then do so, and select **Continue** or press **Enter**.

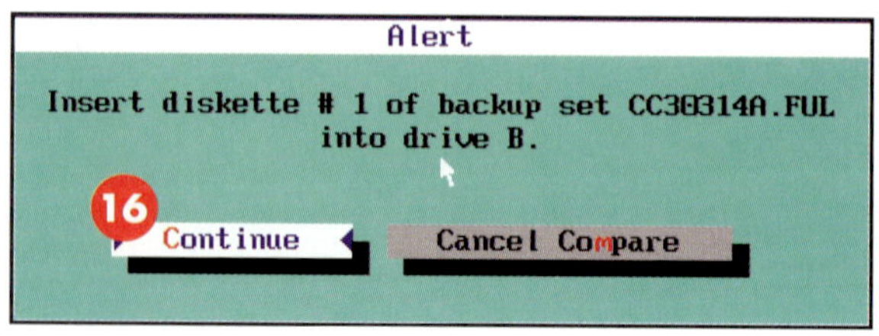

17 Wait until you're told to Insert Disk #2, then do so.

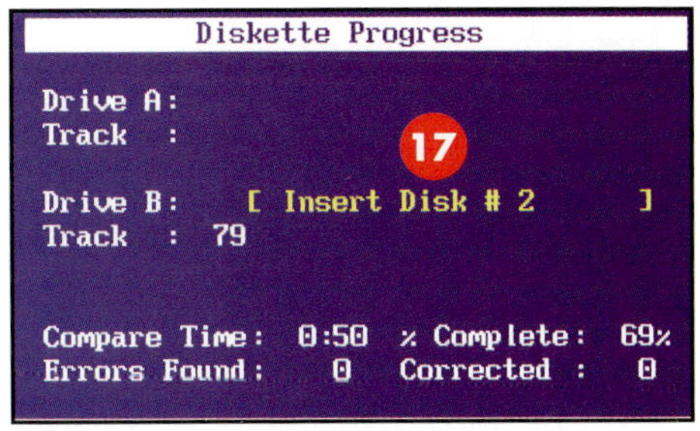

18 Wait for the Compare Complete window to appear, then choose **OK**, or press **Enter** to continue.

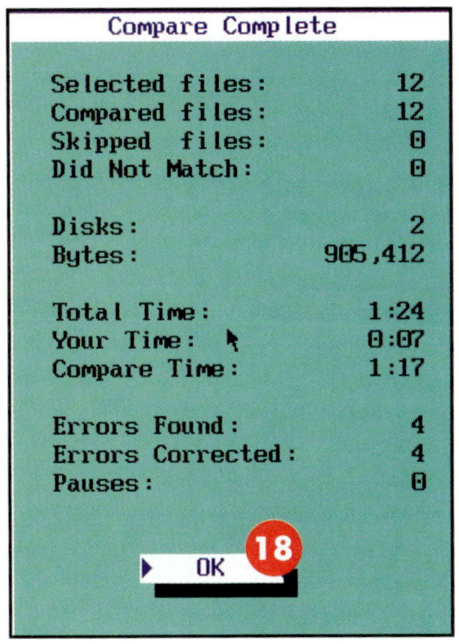

19 At the Compatibility Test box, choose **OK**, or press **Enter**.

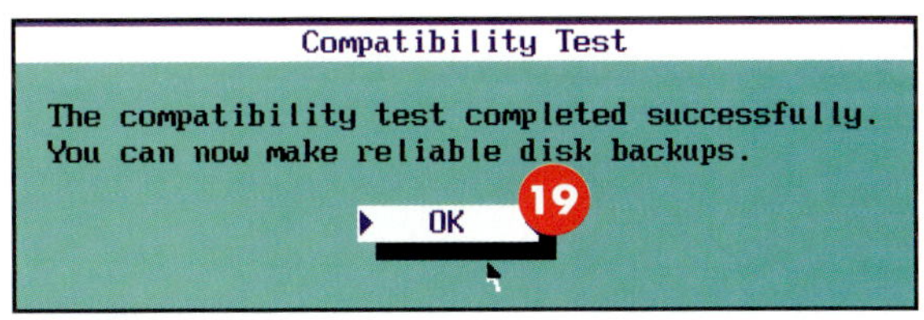

RESTORING FILES TO YOUR HARD DISK

Why Restore Files?

Making a backup is like "saving files for a rainy day." You restore files when it rains. Whenever a file that you once had on your hard disk is no longer there, for whatever reason, you can restore it from the backup you made.

QUICK REFRESHER

As you may remember from working with the DOS Shell, to select something, double-click on it with the mouse, or **Tab** to it, and press **Enter**.

TIP

If *all* your files are gone, then something horrible has probably happened. You'll need to find out what the problem was and correct it, then reinstall DOS from your original diskettes, before you can use this procedure. See the back of this book for instructions on Installing DOS.

Restoring Files

1. Type **MSBACKUP** at the DOS prompt to start MS Backup, and press **Enter**.

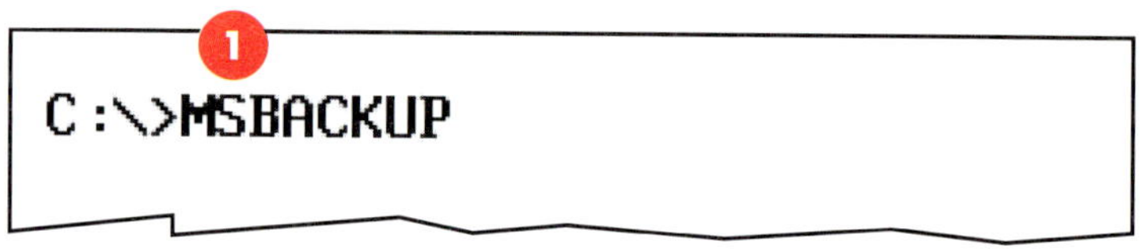

2. Select **R**estore.

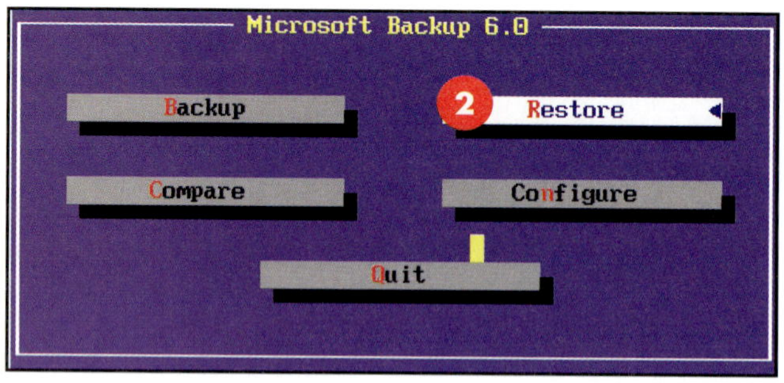

3 The backup catalog that matches your backup disks should be listed under Backup Set Catalog. If it's there, skip to step 7.

4 If the wrong backup set is shown, click on Backup Set Catalog.

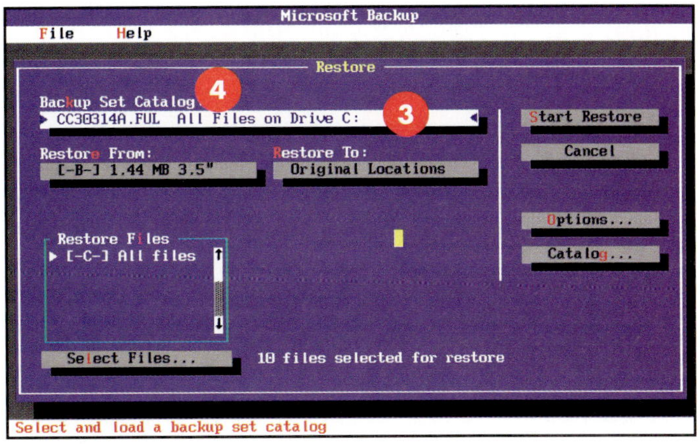

5 Select the catalog you want from the list.

6 Select Load to return to the Restore screen.

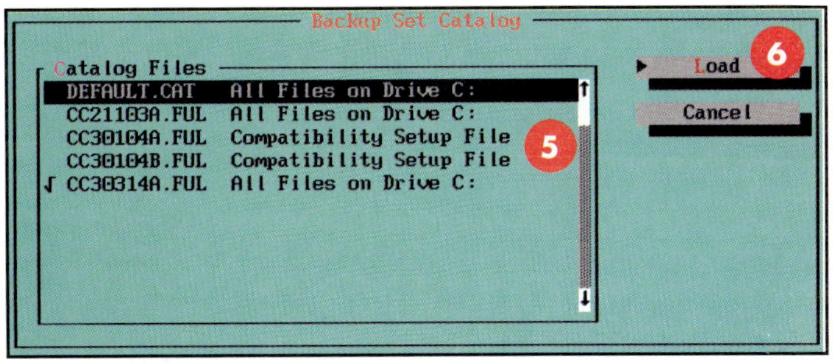

7 If you want to restore all the available files, double-click on the drive letter under Restore Files, or highlight it and press the **Spacebar**. Then skip to step 11.

8 If you want to restore only certain files, choose Select Files.

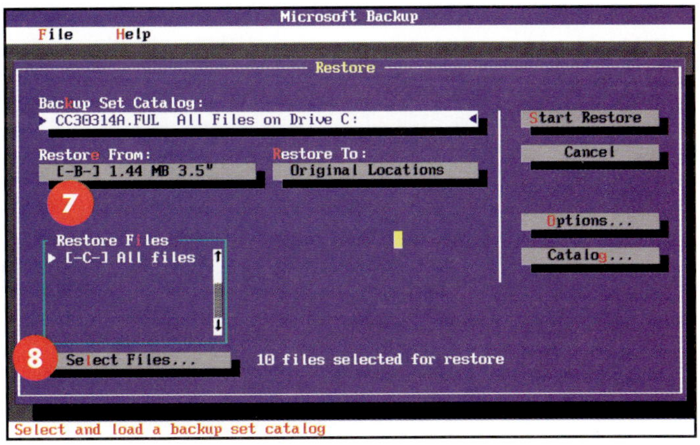

RESTORING FILES TO YOUR HARD DISK

9. Highlight the files and/or directories you want to restore, then press the **Spacebar** to select them.

10. Choose **OK**, or press **Enter** to return to the Restore screen.

Checked files are selected

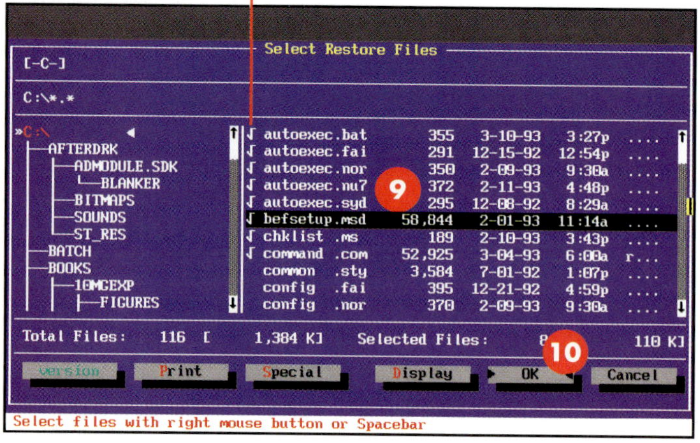

11. Choose **Start Restore**.

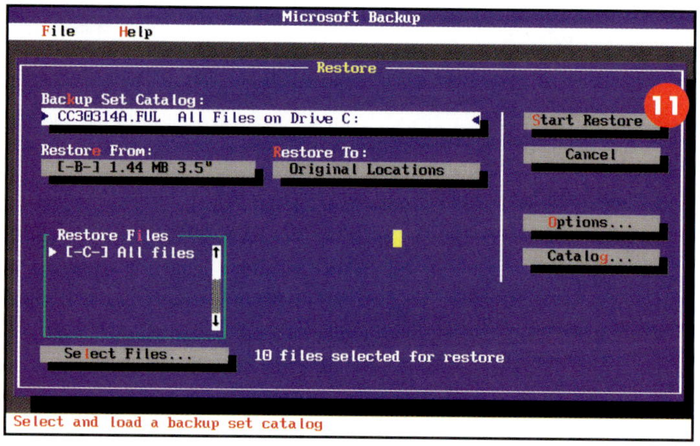

12. When prompted, insert Diskette #1 in the diskette drive and choose **Continue**, or press **Enter**.

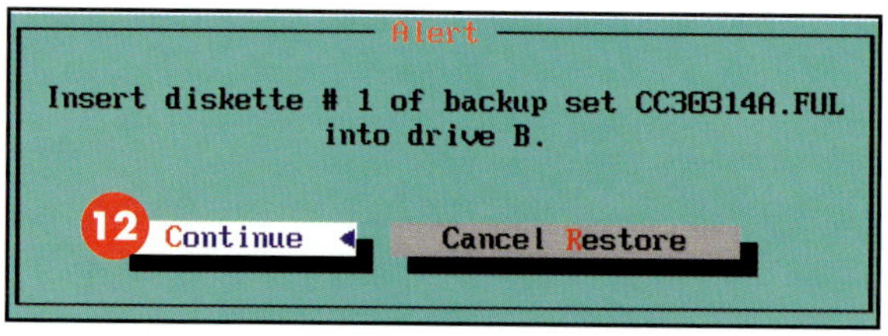

13. If you get a message that the file already exists, choose **Overwrite** to overwrite it or **Do Not Restore** to skip it.

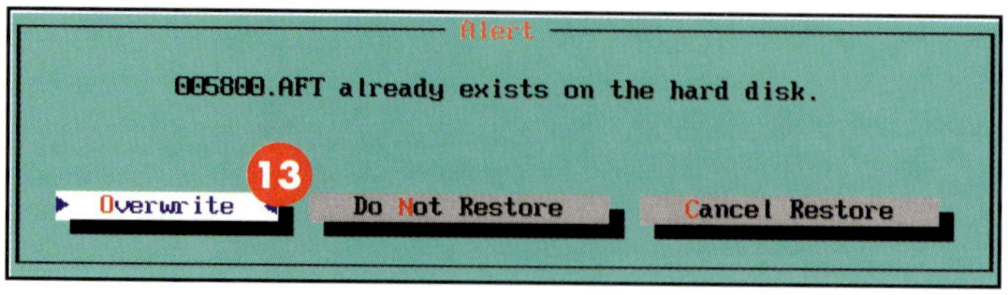

14 When prompted, insert disk #2 in the diskette drive.

15 Continue inserting the disks that are requested.

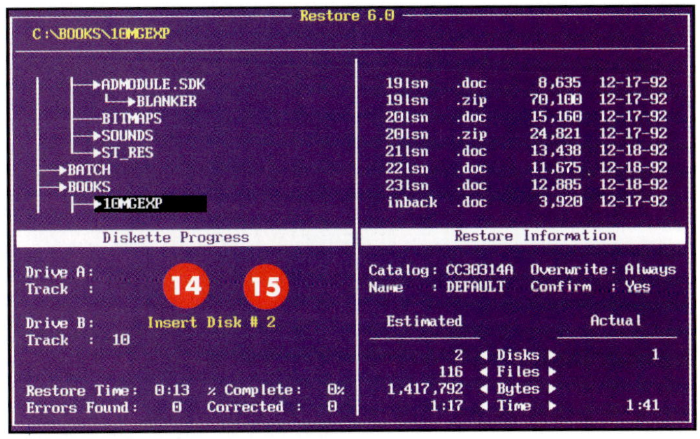

16 When the restoring process is complete, choose **OK**, or press **Enter** to return to the main screen.

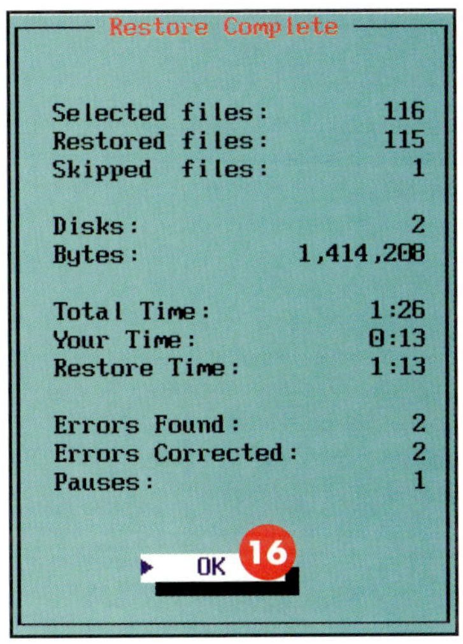

TIP

If no backup sets are shown, you can't continue until you retrieve the catalog from the diskettes. Quit now, and go to the "Retrieving a Backup Catalog" task.

TIP

The file and directory lists in MS Backup are very similar to the Directory Tree and File List in the DOS Shell. If you need to review how to move around in such listings, refer back to the DOS Shell section.

RETRIEVING A BACKUP CATALOG

Why Retrieve a Backup Catalog?

If your hard disk is completely wiped out, obviously all your backup catalogs are wiped out as well. You can reinstall DOS from your original disks, but your backup catalogs, those essential ingredients for a successful restore, are gone forever.

Fortunately, DOS saves a duplicate copy of the backup catalog on the last disk of every set of backup disks. You can easily retrieve it from there.

LEARNING THE LINGO

Backup catalog: A file that contains an index of all the files backed up. MS Backup uses the backup catalog when it restores the files (see the "Restoring Files to your Hard Disk" task).

Retrieving a Backup Catalog

1. If you are not already running MSBACKUP, type **MSBACKUP** and press **Enter**.

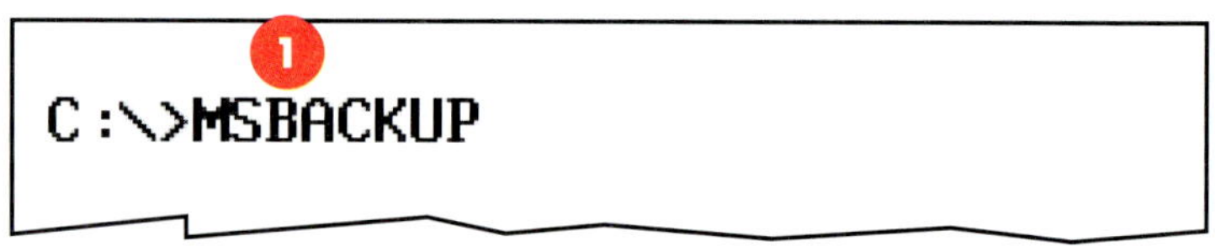

2. From the main MS Backup menu, choose **Restore**.

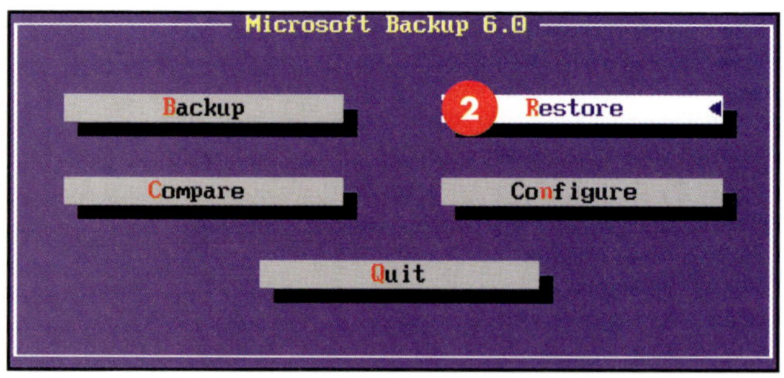

3 Select Catalog.

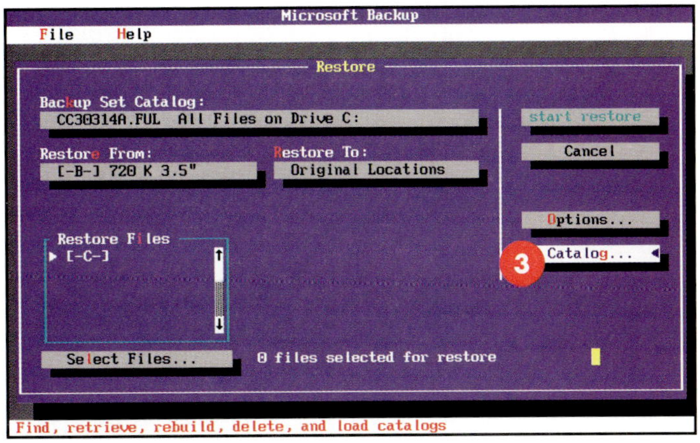

4 Select **Retrieve**.

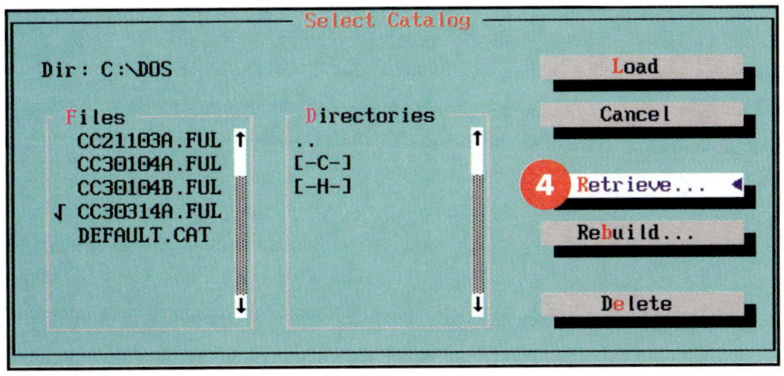

5 Select the floppy drive that fits the backup disks you have (A or B), and select **OK** or press **Enter**.

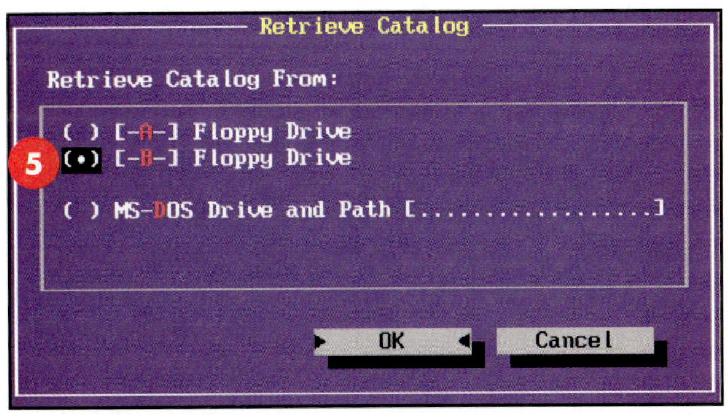

6 When prompted, insert the last disk of the backup set in the disk drive, then select Continue, or press **Enter**.

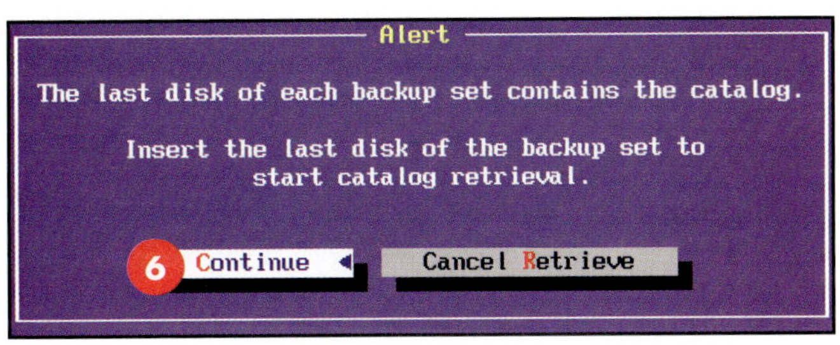

RETRIEVING A BACKUP CATALOG

7 Wait for DOS to retrieve the catalog.

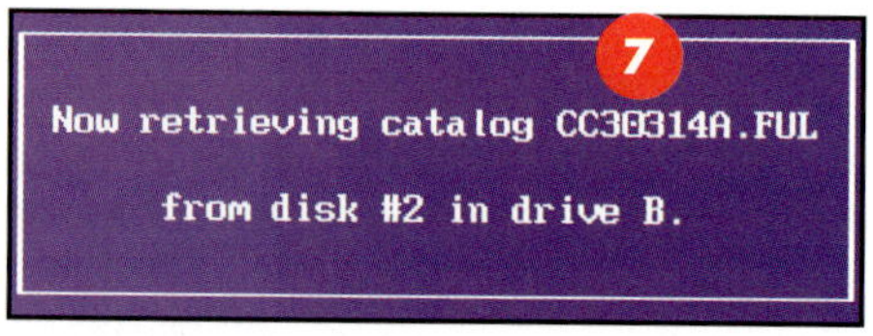

8 When the catalog has been retrieved, choose **OK**, or press **Enter**.

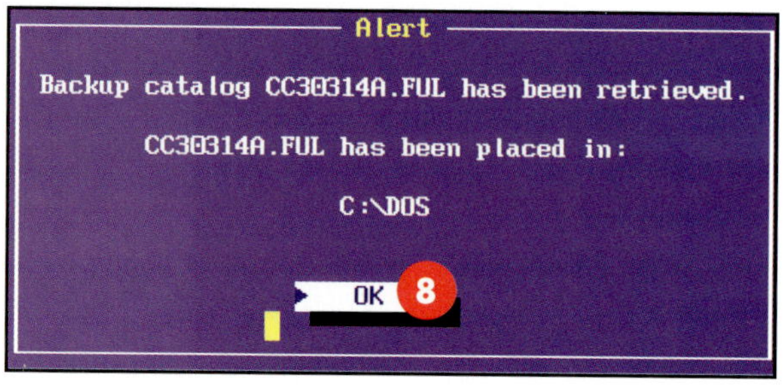

9 Select the retrieved catalog from the **F**iles list.

10 Select **L**oad. You are now ready to return to the "Restoring Files to your Hard Disk" task.

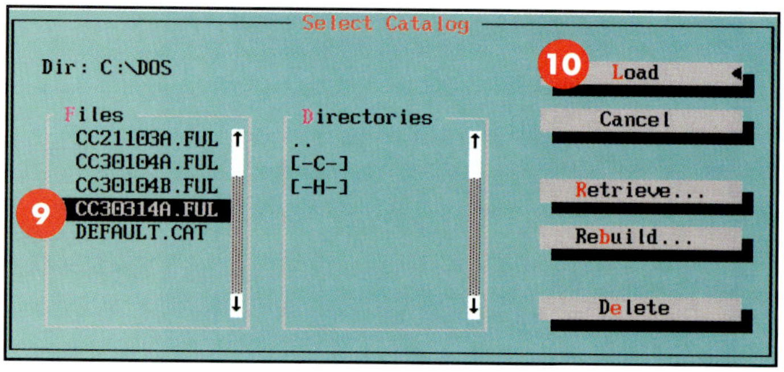

DETECTING COMPUTER VIRUSES

What Is a Virus?

A virus is a sneaky computer program that hides in your computer and then inflicts senseless acts of destruction at some predetermined time, catching you completely off guard. It sounds pretty awful, and it is. You should use MS AntiVirus regularly to guard your system against viruses. MS AntiVirus has two parts: MSAV, which finds and removes viruses, and VSAFE, a memory-resident program that watches for viruses at all times.

TIP

There are several ways your computer can "catch" a virus. An infected floppy disk can pass a virus to your computer and so can an infected file you have downloaded from an electronic bulletin board or information service using a modem. Viruses can also be passed through local area networks (LANs).

LEARNING THE LINGO

Local area network (LAN): A group of computers connected to one another by a cabling system that allows them to share files and directories. There is usually a "server" computer that orchestrates the sharing.

Bulletin board service (BBS): A computer set up to receive phone calls from other computers. The two computers connect through modems to share information and files.

Modem: A device that converts your computer's digital data into analog signals that can be sent through a phone line. Another modem on the other end reverses the process, converting the analog back to digital.

Memory-resident program: A program that runs "in the background" while other programs are running, waiting until it is needed.

Checking for Viruses with MS AntiVirus

1. At the DOS prompt, type **MSAV**, and press **Enter**.

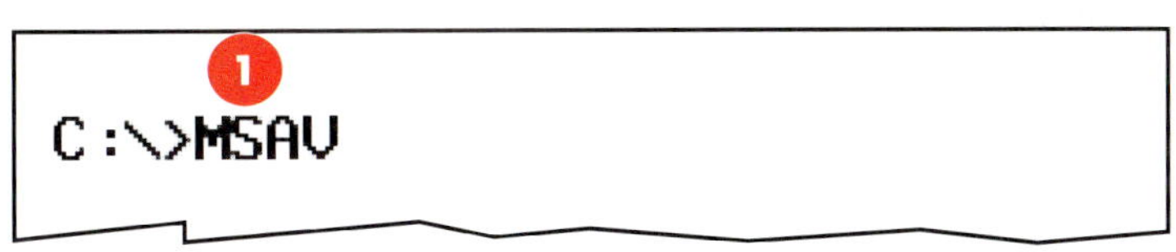

DETECTING COMPUTER VIRUSES

2 Select Detect & **C**lean.

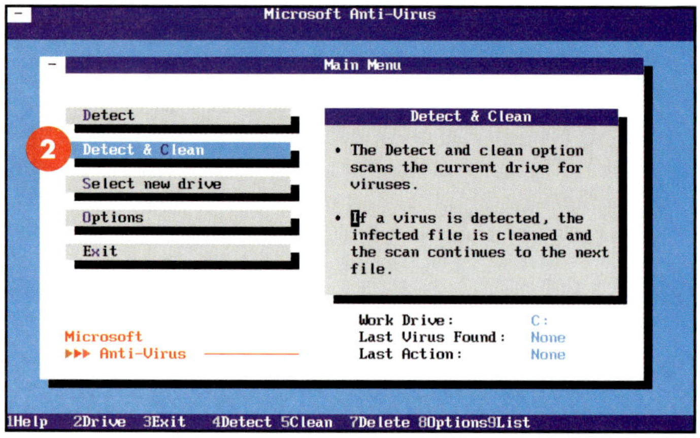

3 Wait for MS Anti-Virus to find viruses or changes to important files.

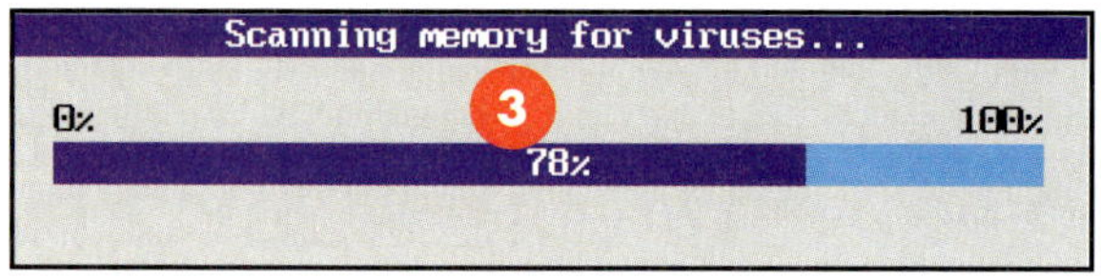

The file that Antivirus is currently examining appears here.

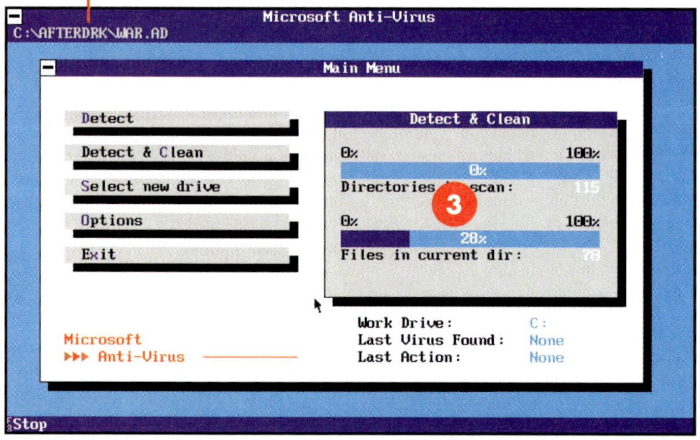

4 If MS AntiVirus finds a file that has changed since it last checked it, choose to **U**pdate AntiVirus's recollection, **R**epair the file, or **C**ontinue without affecting it.

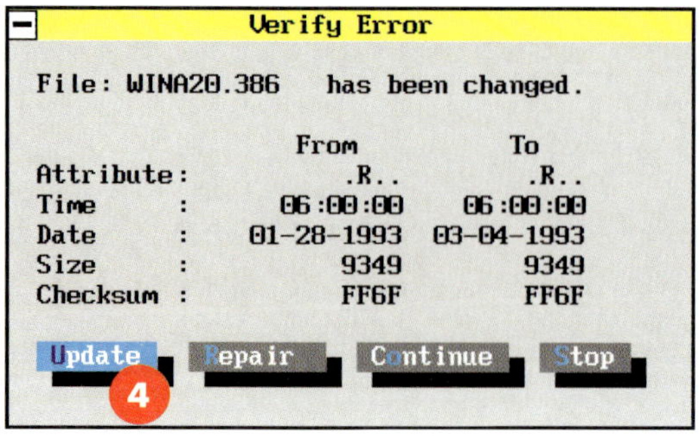

5 When MS AntiVirus is finished, choose **OK**, or press **Enter** to continue.

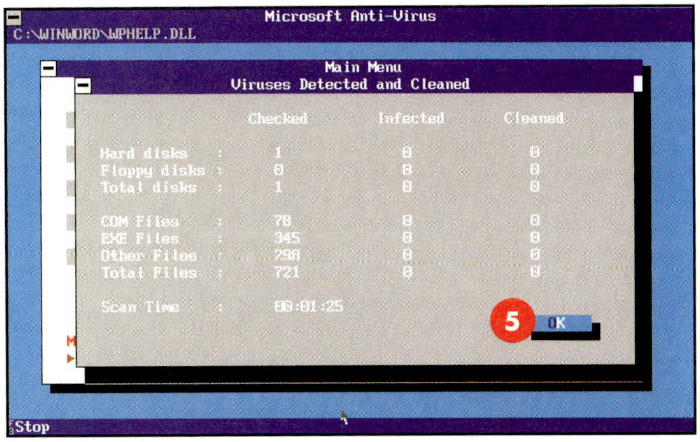

6 Choose Exit to quit the program.

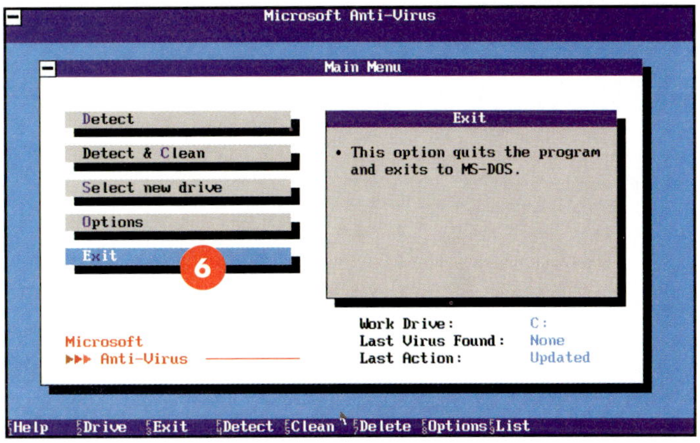

7 Choose **OK**, or press **Enter**.

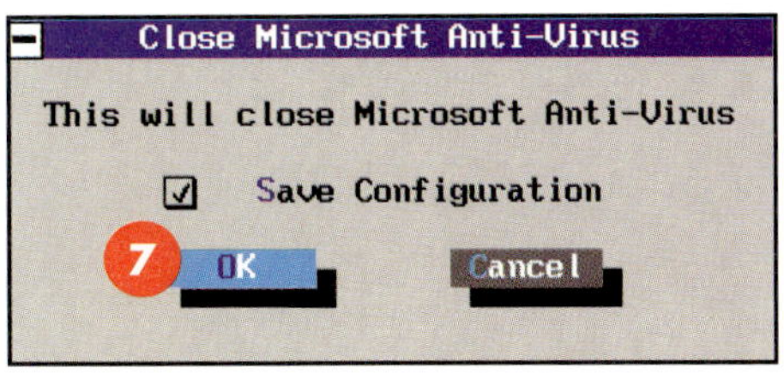

TIP

Unless you strongly suspect foul play on your computer, choose **U**pdate in step 4. Many files change for one reason or another, and it is not normally cause for alarm. However, if MS AntiVirus finds an actual virus (not just a Verify Error), opt to clean it off your system immediately.

DOUBLING YOUR HARD DISK'S CAPACITY WITH DBLSPACE

What Is DBLSPACE?

DoubleSpace, or DBLSPACE, is a data compression program designed to let you fit more data on your hard disk. It stores files more compactly than normal, yet its operation is invisible to you as a user. Once you install DBLSPACE on your hard disk, you can forget it's even there.

LEARNING THE LINGO

Data Compression: The process of storing files more compactly on a disk so the files take up less space.

Installing DBLSPACE

1. At the DOS prompt, type **DBLSPACE**, and press **Enter**.

2. Press **Enter** to set up DoubleSpace now.

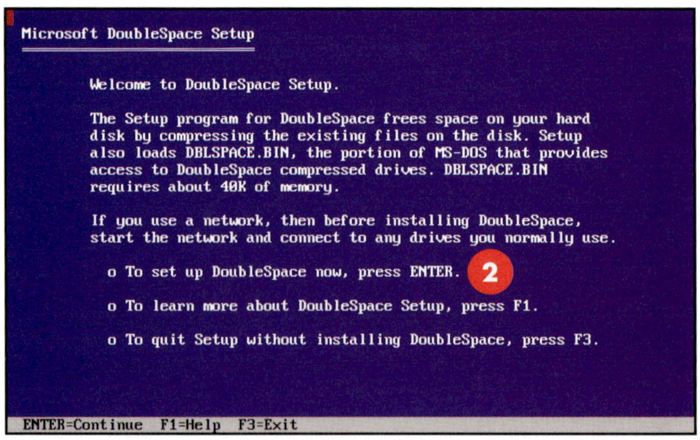

DOUBLING YOUR HARD DISK'S CAPACITY WITH DBLSPACE

3. Press **Enter** to accept Express Setup.

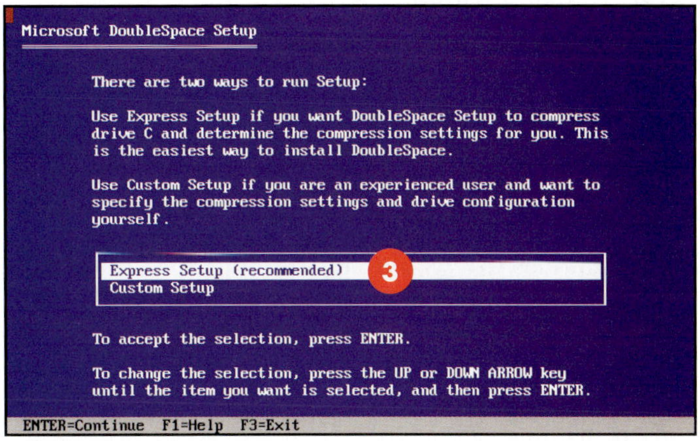

4. To compress the drive, type **C**.

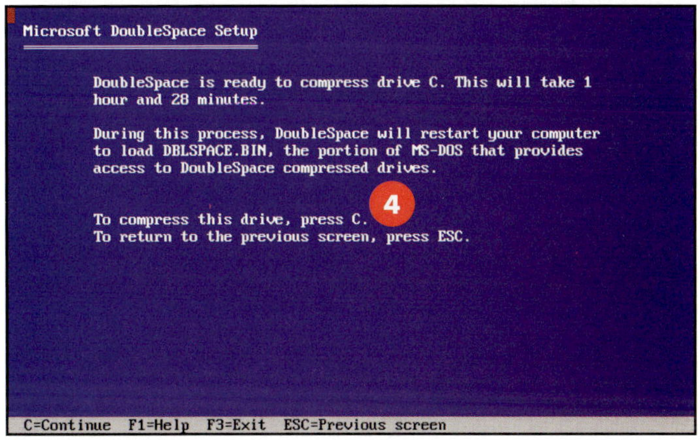

5. Wait as DoubleSpace checks your disk and restarts your computer.

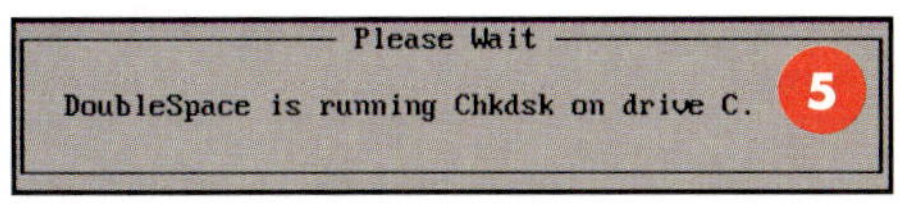

6. At the results screen, press **Enter** to restart your computer.

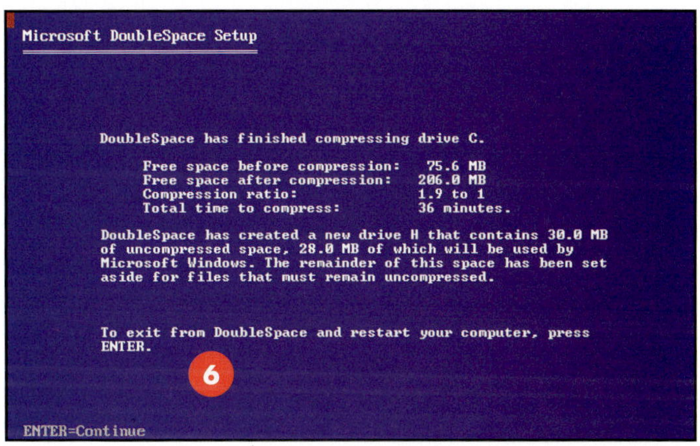

MAXIMIZING YOUR SYSTEM'S MEMORY

Why Maximize Memory?

Your computer has a limited amount of memory, so it's important that your system uses it wisely. With earlier versions of DOS, you could make changes to your startup files that would help save memory, but the procedure was complicated.

With DOS 6, a utility called MEMMAKER automates the process of setting up your computer's memory for maximum performance.

TIP

If you know quite a bit about computer memory, you may want to press **Spacebar** and then **Enter** in step 3 to choose Custom setup. Custom setup allows you to specify advanced options that may help squeeze the last bit of memory from your system. Custom setup is beyond the scope of this book and is not recommended for beginners.

If you know *for certain* that you have programs that need expanded memory, press **Spacebar** and then **Enter** in step 4 to select Yes. Most people, however, don't need it, and the settings required for expanded memory can hinder DOS's use of memory for other purposes.

You can always run MEMMAKER again and specify that you need expanded memory later if you find that you have a program that requires it.

Using MemMaker to Maximize Your Memory

1. Type **MEMMAKER**, and press **Enter**.

2 Press **Enter** to continue.

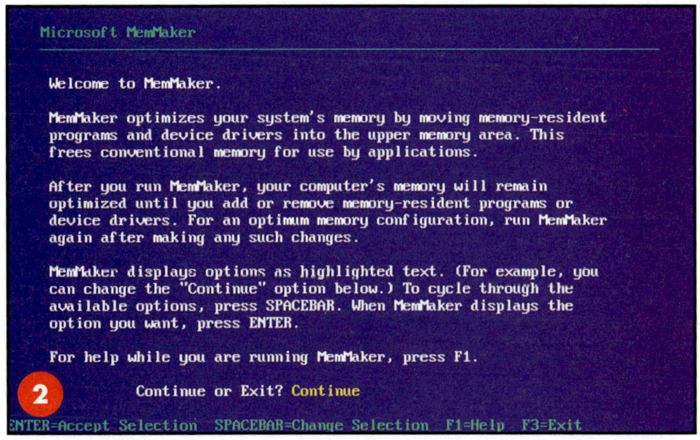

3 Press **Enter** to accept Express Setup.

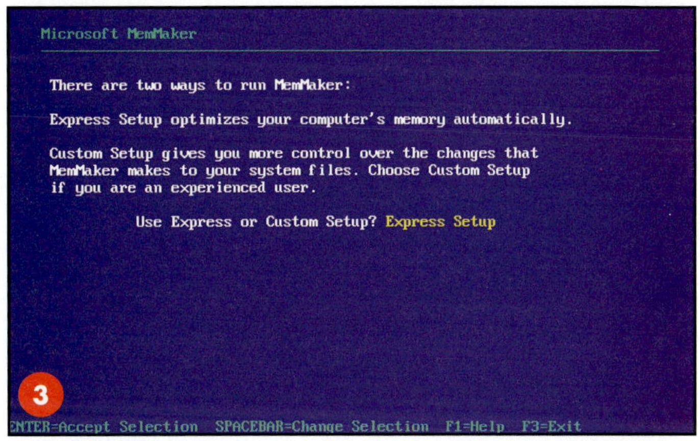

4 Press **Enter** to answer No when asked if you need expanded memory (EMS).

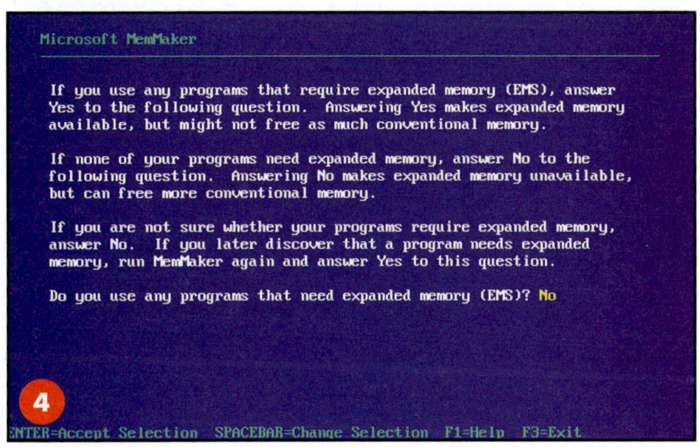

MAXIMIZE YOUR SYSTEM'S MEMORY

5 Press **Enter** to restart your computer.

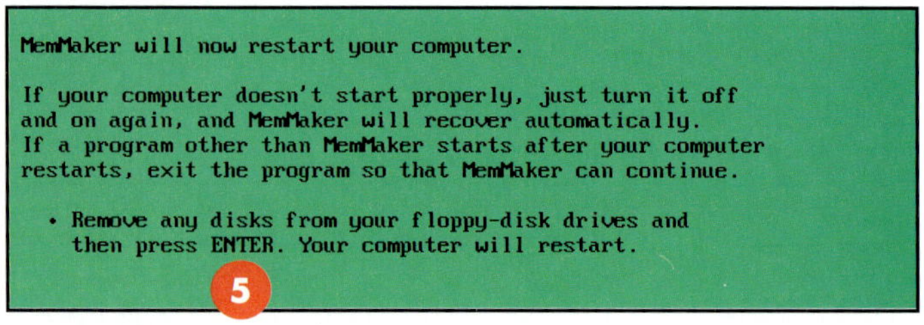

6 Press **Enter** to restart again when prompted.

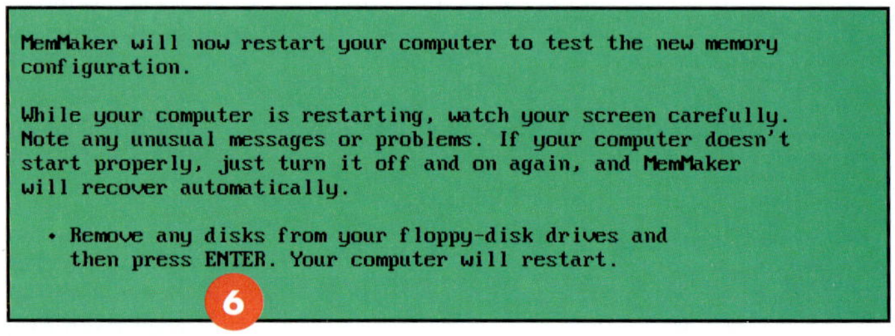

7 If your system restarted with no error messages displayed, press **Enter** to select Yes. If not, press **Spacebar** then **Enter**.

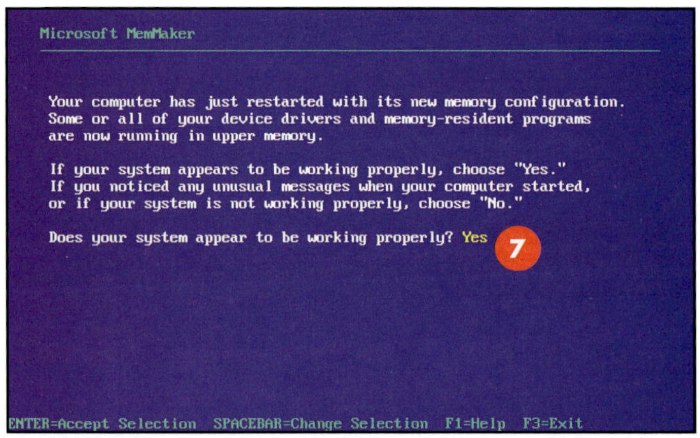

8 Press **Enter** to exit and save the changes that MemMaker made, or press **Esc** to exit and discard MemMaker's changes.

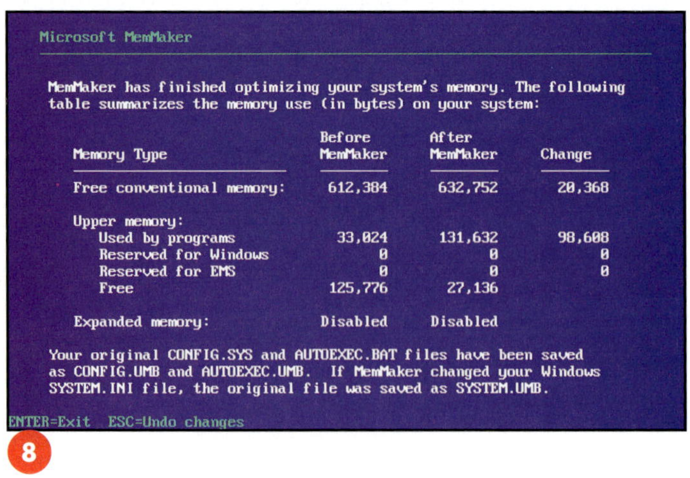

Installing DOS 6

Before you can use DOS 6, you must first install it on your computer, unless your computer came with DOS 6 preinstalled. Luckily, the setup procedure is very intuitive. Just follow along with the screen prompts.

TIP

If a version of DOS is not already installed on your computer, place DISK 1 of the DOS installation disks in drive A:, then turn on your computer's power. You can then join in the following setup procedure at step 6.

Some Things to Know Before You Start

During installation, DOS will ask you what kind of monitor you have (EGA, VGA, and so on) and where your current DOS files are kept (usually in a directory called C:\DOS). Have this information handy.

DOS will also ask you whether you want to install utility programs for DOS only, Windows only, or DOS and Windows. DOS will try to guess what you want; here are my recommendations:

- If DOS chooses DOS Only, it means that it could not find a copy of Microsoft Windows on your computer. If you don't use Windows, accept DOS Only. If you do, change to DOS and Windows.
- If DOS chooses Windows Only, it means that DOS found Microsoft Windows on your computer. If you are going to follow along with the steps in Part III of this book, you should change to DOS and Windows, because the screens in this book are based on the DOS versions of the utilities.

Installing DOS 6

1. Insert Disk 1 of the DOS installation disks in either drive A: or B:.

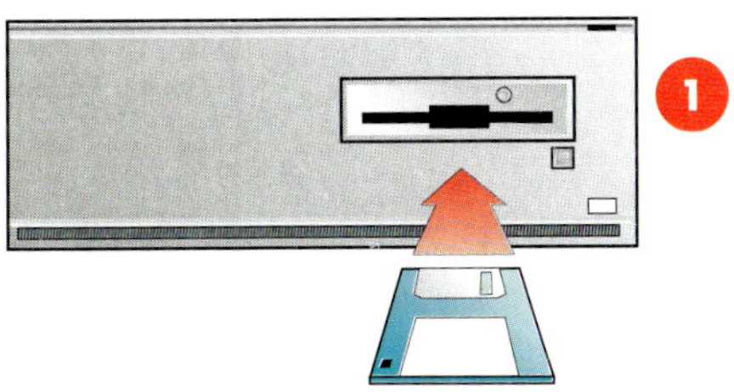

2 At the DOS prompt, type the drive letter containing the disk followed by a colon (for example, A: or B:). Then type **SETUP**.

3 Press **Enter**.

4 At the Welcome screen, press **Enter** to continue.

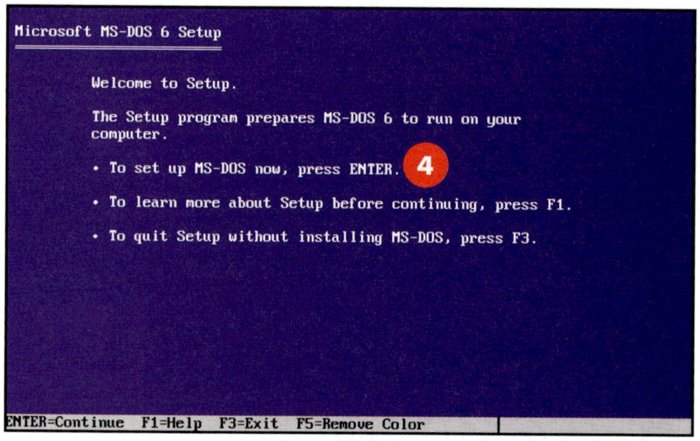

5 Find and label one or two floppy disks as directed on the screen, and press **Enter**.

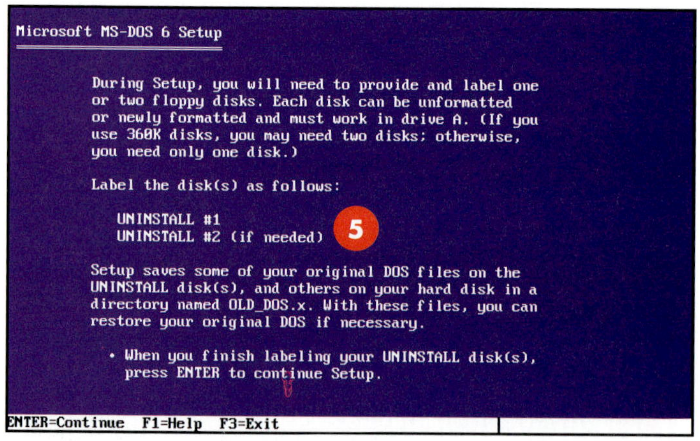

6 Examine the settings DOS has picked for you. If they are correct (or if you aren't sure), press **Enter** to continue, then skip to step 9.

7 If a setting is incorrect, use the arrow keys to highlight it, then press **Enter**.

8 From the list of options for that setting, use the arrow keys to highlight a different one, then press **Enter** and return to step 6.

9 Examine the list of utility programs DOS has picked for you. If they are what you want, press **Enter** to continue, then skip to step 12.

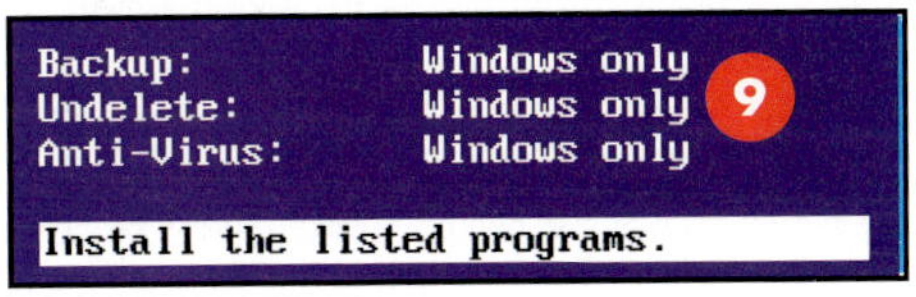

10 If you want a different version of a utility installed, use the arrow keys to highlight the current setting, then press **Enter**.

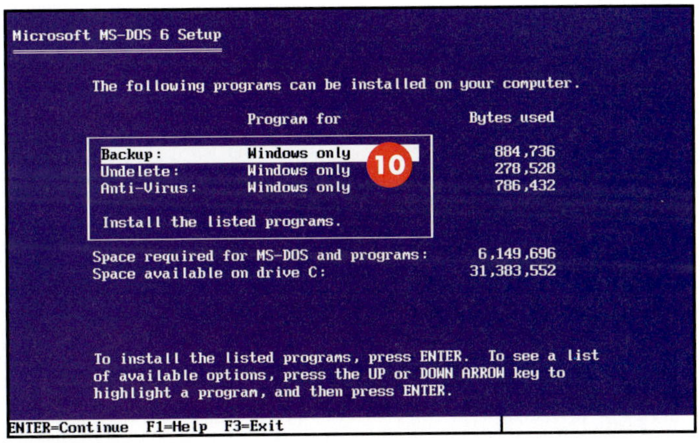

11 From the list, use the arrow keys to highlight the version you want, then press **Enter** and return to step 9.

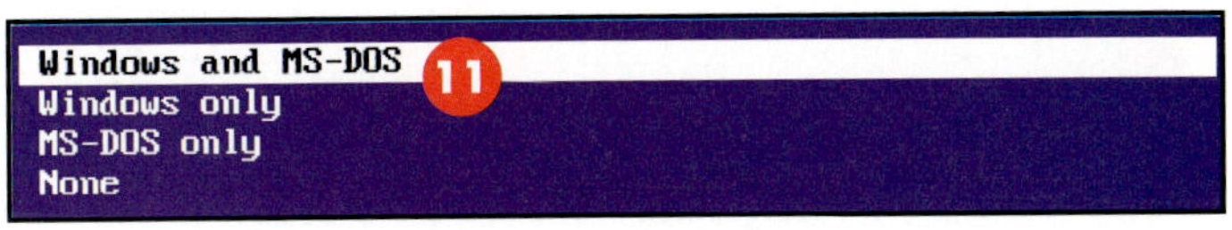

12 If DOS says it has found Windows, press **Enter** to accept Windows' location.

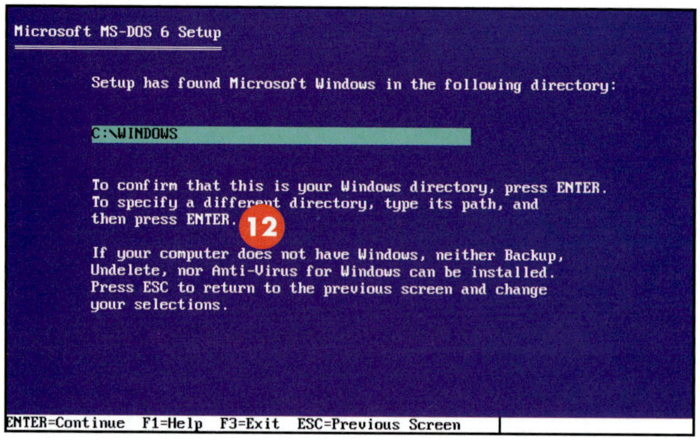

13 Press **Y** to install DOS.

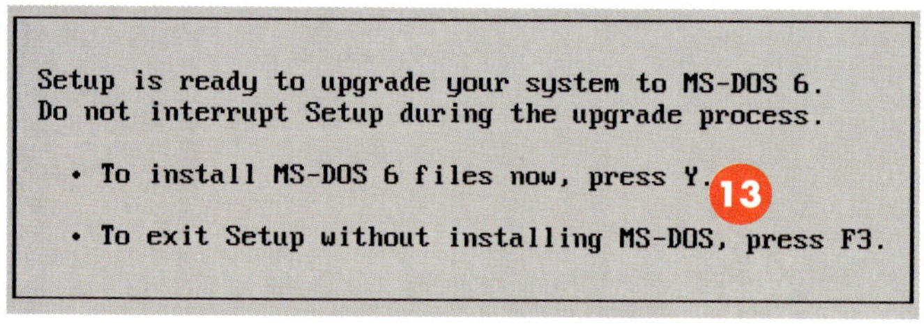

14 Insert the disk you labeled UNINSTALL #1 into drive A:, and press **Enter**.

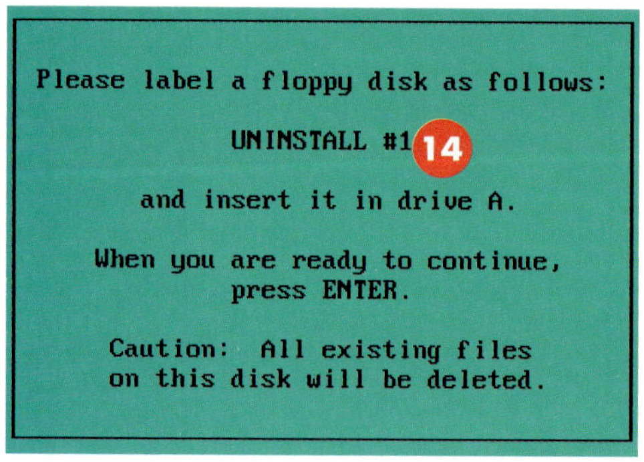

TIP

If your computer does not restart correctly, put the UNINSTALL #1 disk in drive A:. Hold down the **Ctrl** and **Alt** keys, and press the **Del** key. An uninstall program will run that will allow you to restore your old version of DOS.

15. When prompted, insert the installation disks that DOS needs into the drive that DOS specifies, and press **Enter**.

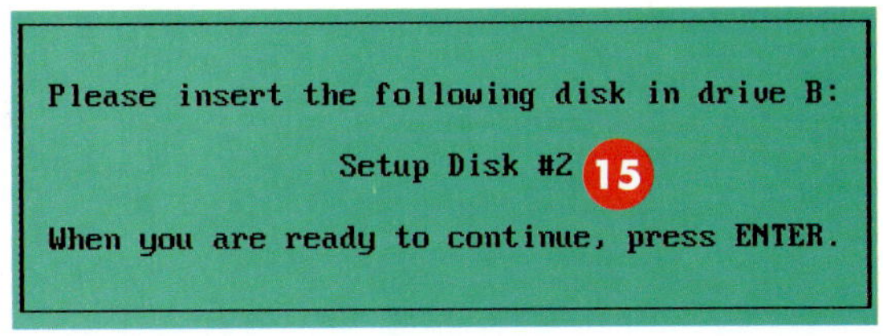

16. When prompted, remove all the disks and press **Enter**.

17. When prompted, press **Enter** again to restart your system.

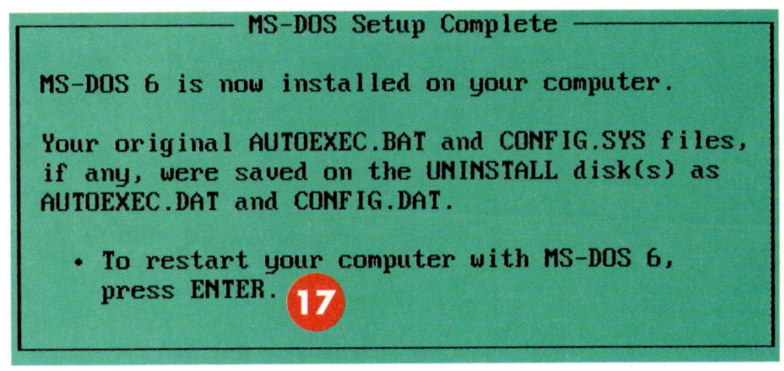

TIP

If DOS 6 is up and running files, you can delete the files from your hard disk that make uninstallation possible. Just type **DELOLDOS** at the DOS prompt, and follow the on-screen instructions.

DOS Error Messages

DOS error messages can be frustrating when you're just starting out. They're cryptic, and abrupt, and often they don't give you a clue as to how to fix the problem. Use this section as your "quick fix" when you encounter an error message.

Access denied

What happened:

You tried to delete a file that is protected.

What you should do now:

You should probably not delete this file, since files are protected for a reason. If you feel that you need to delete this file, ask a PC guru for advice.

Bad command or filename

What happened (1):

You mistyped the command.

What you should do now:

Check the spelling of the command and any file name. Verify that you did not enter extra spaces where they are not needed.

What happened (2):

The command you are trying to use is an external command, and DOS does not recognize it.

What you should do now:

Type **PATH**, and verify that **C:\DOS** is a part of the path. See Part II for more information on setting up a PATH for DOS to follow.

What happened (3):

You might have tried to start a program that lives in a directory DOS can't find. The directory might not exist anymore.

What you should do now:

Move to the program directory by typing something like this: **CD\PROGRAM**. If you use this program a lot, you may want to add the program's directory to your DOS path. See Part II for more information on how to setup a PATH for DOS to follow.

Bad or missing command interpreter

What happened (1):

You've just exited a program that you started from a diskette.

What you should do now:

You should not remove a diskette that a program is using. Reinsert the disk that you started the program from or reboot the computer (press **Ctrl**, **Alt**, and **Delete** at the same time), and it should be okay.

What happened (2):

The COMMAND.COM file that is normally in the root directory of your drive C has been accidentally deleted, or while copying all the files from a diskette, you've copied an older version of the COMMAND.COM file onto your drive.

What you should do now:

Reboot the computer (press **Ctrl+Alt+Delete**) with your emergency diskette in drive A. Type this: **COPY A:COMMAND.COM C:**.

Bad sectors

What happened:

After formatting a diskette, a number of bad sectors may be displayed. The diskette may simply be damaged, or you may have formatted the diskette to the wrong density.

What you should do now:

Verify that you formatted the disk to the proper density.

Current drive is no longer valid

What happened:

You removed a diskette before a function was complete, or you were trying to use a diskette drive that didn't have a disk in it.

What you should do now:

Put the disk in the disk drive. If you wish to make drive A the current drive, type **A:** at the prompt. If you wish to return to drive C, type **C:** at the prompt.

Data error reading drive *x*

What happened:

A file is damaged.

What you should do now:

Press **R** for Retry. If that doesn't work and the message returns, press **A** for Abort. Try to locate another copy of the file (say on a backup) and use it instead. If the file is on a diskette, try reinserting the diskette in its drive. If you have any disk utilities, such as Norton Utilities, they might be able to repair a damaged disk.

Duplicate file name or file not found

What happened:

You were using the REN command to rename a file, but the new file name already exists.

What you should do now:

Try the command with another name, as in **REN OLDFILE.DOC NEWFILE.DOC**.

Errors found, F parameter not specified

What happened:

You used the CHKDSK command but did not include the /F switch. Errors on the hard disk were found.

What you should do now:

Retype the command as **CHKDSK /F**. When asked, type **Y** to convert lost clusters and chains to files.

Error reading drive x

See *General failure error reading drive x*.

File cannot be copied onto itself

What happened:

When using the COPY command, you either didn't specify a new path for the file or a new name.

What you should do now:

If you typed something like **COPY JENNY.DOC**, DOS doesn't know what to do. Copy JENNY.DOC where? If you want to copy the file into the current directory, do you want to give it a new name? Be sure to specify complete paths when copying a file, as in **COPY JENNY.DOC A:** or **COPY JENNY.DOC NEWJENNY.DOC**.

File not found

What happened (1):

You mistyped the file name in the command.

What you should do now:

Retype the command with the correct file name. If necessary, type **DIR /P** to verify the spelling of the file name.

What happened (2):

You mistyped the path leading to the file.

What you should do now:

Verify the path you are using, and make sure that you type a backslash (\) to separate the parts of a path, as in **C:\PROJECTS\DRU\CHAP01.DOC**.

What happened (3):

The file you referenced in the command does not exist.

What you should do now:

Try the command again, with a different file.

General failure error reading drive x. Abort, Retry, Fail?

What happened (1):

If the referenced drive is a diskette drive, there may not be a diskette in the drive, or the drive door is not closed.

What you should do now:

Place a diskette in the drive, and make sure that the drive door is closed. Press **R** for retry.

What happened (2):

The diskette in the referenced drive might not be formatted.

What you should do now:

Press **F** for Fail, then format the diskette to its proper density by typing something like **FORMAT A: /V**.

What happened (3):

The diskette in the referenced drive is damaged and cannot be read.

What you should do now:

Replace with another diskette, and press **R** for Retry, or press **F** for Fail, and reformat this diskette.

What happened (4):

The diskette in the referenced drive may not be placed in the drive properly.

What you should do now:

Remove the diskette from its drive, and verify that it is placed properly within the drive. If necessary, tap the diskette on the side to make sure that the diskette material has not shifted in the sleeve.

What happened (5):

There is a possibility that the referenced drive is having problems. If you are trying to use the hard disk, this could be the first indicator of some major problems.

What you should do now:

Have a PC guru help you test your hard disk.

What happened (6):

If you are trying to start a program, this could indicate a problem with the program files. If you get this error with a variety of programs, the problem is more likely your hard disk.

What you should do now:

Again, have a PC guru help you test your hard disk. They may recommend re-installing the program.

Insufficient disk space

What happened:

You tried to copy a file onto a diskette, and there is not enough room.

What you should do now:

Delete some files from the diskette to make room for the files you want, or reuse the COPY command with another diskette.

Insufficient memory

What happened:

You are trying to start a program, and you get this message. You have too many things in memory (RAM), and you need to unload some of them.

What you should do now:

Exit as many programs as possible, then retry the command. If necessary, reboot the computer; rebooting (pressing **Ctrl+Alt+Delete**) causes a computer's memory to clear. You might want to take steps to improve memory usage; see Part III to learn about MemMaker, a utility that can help.

Invalid directory

What happened (1):

You are trying to change to a directory that does not exist, or you've misspelled the directory name.

What you should do now:

Check the spelling of the directory. If you have at least DOS 5, type **DIR C:*. /S** to display a listing of directories on your hard disk.

What happened (2):

You forgot to place a backslash between a directory and a subdirectory name.

What you should do now:

Remember to use a backslash (\) to separate the parts of a path name, as in **C:\WORD\DOCS**.

Invalid drive specification

What happened (1):

You referenced a drive that does not exist.

What you should do now:

Type a valid drive letter.

What happened (2):

You referenced a network drive on to which you are not yet logged.

What you should do now:

Log on to the network drive, then repeat the original command.

Invalid file name or file not found

What happened (1):

You used the TYPE command with wild cards, as in TYPE *.BAT.

What you should do now:

You can only use the TYPE command on a single file name, as in **TYPE AUTOEXEC.BAT**.

What happened (2):

You tried to rename a file to an invalid file name.

What you should do now:

Try renaming the file to something else.

Invalid media or Track 0 Bad

What happened:

You're trying to format a diskette to the wrong density, or the diskette is badly damaged.

What you should do now:

Verify the density of the diskette, and try formatting it again.

Invalid parameter or Invalid switch

What happened (1):

You used a parameter or switch that is invalid for this command.

What you should do now:

Check the appropriate task in this book, and follow the steps carefully.

What happened (2):

You entered a space between the forward slash and the character when entering a switch.

What you should do now:

If you want to enter a switch for a command, such as the /W switch for the DIR command (which tells the DIR command to display files in a wide format), do not type a space between the forward slash (/) and the W. Type the command like this: **DIR /W** and not like this: DIR / W.

What happened (3):

You used a backward slash when specifying a switch.

What you should do now:

Use a forward slash for switches, as in **DIR /W** and not DIR \W.

What happened (4):

You used a forward slash when specifying a file name path.

What you should do now:

Use a backward slash (\) when specifying the path to a file, as in **C:\WORD\NEW.DOC**.

Invalid path

What happened:

You specified an incorrect path to a file, or you mistyped a directory name.

What you should do now:

Verify the path and retype the command.

Invalid path, not directory, or directory not empty

What happened (1):

You used the RD command to remove a directory, and that directory contains subdirectories or files.

What you should do now:

Delete the files and subdirectories first, then repeat the RD command. If you use DOS 6, you can use the DELTREE command instead. See Part II for more information.

What happened (2):

You used the RD command to remove a directory, and the path you typed is invalid.

What you should do now:

Check the path to the directory you are trying to delete. Remember to use a backslash (\) to separate the parts of a path, as in **C:\WORD\DOCS**.

Non-System disk or disk error. Replace and press any key when ready

What happened:

Leaving a diskette in drive A while you boot the computer.

What you should do now:

Remove the diskette and press **Ctrl+Alt+Delete** at the same time. Do not press "any key to continue," as the screen suggests, because you run the risk of transmitting a virus to your system if the diskette is infected.

Not ready reading drive x. Abort, Retry, Fail?

What happened:

You've typed a command which references a diskette drive, and there is no diskette in that drive.

What you should do now:

Place a diskette in the drive, then press **R** for Retry. If you no longer wish to execute the command, press **A** for Abort.

Press any key to continue...

What happened:

This is not an error message. DOS is pausing while it waits for you to do something, such as switch diskettes in a drive, or read the display.

What you should do now:

When you are ready to continue, you can press any key on the keyboard, such as the Enter key. Do not look for a key called "Any," although it sounds as if there should be a specific key you should press, you can actually press any key you want.

Required parameter missing

What happened:

You left out some required part of a command.

What you should do now:

Refer to the appropriate task in this book, and follow the examples closely.

Source diskette bad or incompatible

What happened:

When using the DISKCOPY command, you specified two diskette drives of different densities.

What you should do now:

If the two diskette drives are different densities, you'll have to use one drive to do your disk copying, as in **DISKCOPY B: B:**.

Specified drive does not exist or is non-removeable

What happened (1):

When using the DISKCOPY command, you specified a hard disk drive.

What you should do now:

Use only diskette drive letters with the DISKCOPY command, as in **DISKCOPY A: A:**.

What happened (2):

When using the DISKCOPY command, you specified a nonexistent drive.

What you should do now:

Make sure you specify valid drive letters.

Warning: all data on non-removable disk drive *x*: will be lost! Proceed with Format (Y/N)?

What happened:

You used the FORMAT command and did not specify a drive, or you specified a hard disk drive.

What you should do now:

Retype the FORMAT command with a diskette drive specified, as in **FORMAT B:**.

Write protect error writing drive *x*

What happened:

You're trying to copy data onto a protected diskette.

What you should do now:

If you really want to do this, remove the write protect tab (if it's a 5 1/4-inch diskette) or move the write-protect switch to cover the "hole" (if its a 3 1/2-inch diskette), then press **R** for Retry. If you don't want to copy the file, press **A** for Abort.

Glossary

I've tried to define terms in the book wherever they came up, but there are many computer terms out there. This glossary can help you make sense of them, not only the ones in this book but some others that you may hear bandied about as you meet other computer users. When you encounter a word you don't understand, don't be intimidated—just look it up!

active area The area of the screen where the cursor is currently located. You can quickly spot the active area because it changes color or shading.

active directory The directory that DOS is working with at the moment. DOS can work with only one directory at a time. The directory whose name is highlighted on the Directory Tree. The active directory's files appear on the File List.

active drive The disk drive for which files and directories are currently showing on-screen.

application Also known as program, a set of instructions that enable a computer to perform a specific task, such as word processing or data management.

AUTOEXEC.BAT A special file that contains commands that are automatically executed when your computer is booted.

backing up A process that copies your files onto diskettes in a special compressed format. If something bad happens to the originals, you can restore your backed-up files (a process that uncompresses the files and copies them back).

backup catalog A file that contains an index of all the files backed up. MS Backup uses the backup catalog when restoring the files (see the "Restoring Files to your Hard Disk" task).

boot To start up a computer. The term comes from "pull up by the bootstraps."

bulletin board service (BBS) A computer set up to receive phone calls from other computers. The two computers connect through modems to share information and files.

byte A byte is the amount of space it takes to store one character, such as 1, Q, or $. A byte is made up of eight bits; for example, the byte 01000001 represents the letter A.

click To click on something, position the mouse pointer over the item, then press and release the left mouse button once quickly.

command An "action verb" telling DOS what action you want it to take.

compressed drive A drive whose storage capacity has increased because it uses a more effective method (than just DOS alone) of managing disk space.

configuration The process of setting up a program to work with your particular model of computer and to work according to your preferences.

CONFIG.SYS A file that customizes your PC for the specific programs that you use by changing the system default values for certain parameters. The commands in the CONFIG.SYS file are executed automatically at system startup.

contiguous Files that are grouped together. For example, the words in this sentence are contiguous, but the occurrences of the word "the" in this paragraph are noncontiguous, because there are other words separating them.

cursor The highlight or underline on-screen that tells you "where you are."

data A computer term for information. You enter facts and figures (data) into a computer that then processes it and displays it in an organized manner. In common usage, data and information are used interchangeably.

data compression The process of storing files more compactly on a disk so the files take up less space.

defragmenting The process of collecting all the parts of a file from a disk and rewriting them onto the disk so that all pieces are together in the same spot.

dialog box A dialog box is a special window or box that appears when the program requires additional information before executing a command.

directory A subsection of a disk. Dividing your disk into directories helps you keep track of files. Files with a similar purpose or format can be grouped together in directories.

disk A magnetic computer storage medium. See *floppy disks* and *hard disk*.

disk drive A device that writes data to a magnetic disk and reads data from the disk. Think of a disk drive as a cassette recorder/player. Just as the cassette player can record sounds on a magnetic cassette tape and play back those sounds, a disk drive can record data on a magnetic disk and play back that data.

disk errors Discrepancies between what the disk's File Allocation Table (FAT) thinks is written on the disk and what is actually written.

diskette Another name for floppy disk.

DOS (disk operating system) DOS, which rhymes with "boss," is an essential program that provides the necessary instructions for the computer's parts to function as a unit (keyboard, disk drive, central processing unit, display screen, printer, and so on). DOS interprets the commands you give your computer. Like a traffic cop, DOS controls the flow of information to each computer component.

DOS prompt A group of characters on the left side of the screen, followed by a blinking underline. The DOS prompt indicates that DOS is ready to receive your next command.

DOS Shell A graphics-based program that lets you work with colorful menus and prompts rather than the regular DOS screen.

double-click To move the mouse pointer over an object or icon and press and release the mouse button twice in quick succession.

drag To drag the mouse, first move the mouse to the starting position. Now click and hold the mouse button. Drag the mouse to the ending position and then release the mouse button.

drive A part of your PC that "plays" disks, like your record player plays records. Drives are labeled with letters (A, B, C, and so on).

extension In DOS, each file you create has a unique name. The name consists of two parts: a file name and an extension. The file name can be up to eight characters. The extension (which is optional) can be up to three characters. The extension normally denotes the file type.

file A collection of data that DOS keeps organized under a single name. For example, a letter, a spreadsheet, a text editing program, and a setup utility would each be a file. File names have two parts: a main name, up to eight characters, and then an extension, up to three characters. The two parts are separated by a period, for example, FILENAME.EXT.

File Allocation Table (FAT) A hidden part of the disk where a master list is kept, telling where each file is stored.

file specification When you use wild card characters to specify which files you want a command to act upon, you create a file specification. For example, *.DOC is a file specification. BACKUP.DOC is not a file specification because it contains no * or ?; it's just a file name.

floppy disks Small, portable, plastic storage squares that magnetically store data (the facts and figures you enter and save). Floppy disks are inserted into your computer's floppy disk drive (located on the front of the computer).

formatting A process that prepares a diskette for use. Formatting creates invisible tracks (circles) and sectors (pie shaped wedges) on the surface of the diskette, creating a "map" that DOS can use for keeping track of where files are stored. The number of tracks and sectors that a diskette is divided into will determine how much information it can store.

fragmented file A file whose parts are not all stored in one place on a disk.

function keys The 10 or 12 F keys on the left side of the keyboard or 12 F keys at the top of the keyboard. F keys are numbered F1, F2, F3, and so on. These keys are used to enter various commands in a program.

graphical environment A program that includes boxes, pictures, and other shapes, in addition to plain text. Sometimes called a graphical interface.

graphics mode A way of displaying a program on-screen that includes graphics (that is, pictures, boxes, and other elements besides text). Graphics mode is attractive but some older monitors cannot use it.

hard disk A nonremoveable disk drive that stores many megabytes of data. Because it is fixed inside the computer, it performs quicker and more efficiently than a floppy disk.

kilobyte A unit for measuring the amount of data. A kilobyte is equivalent to 1,024 bytes.

local area network (LAN) A group of computers connected to one another by a cabling system that allows them to share files and directories. There is usually a "server" computer that orchestrates the sharing.

megabyte A standard unit used to measure the storage capacity of a disk and the amount of computer memory. A megabyte is 1,048,576 bytes (1,000 kilobytes). This is roughly equivalent to 500 pages of double-spaced text. Megabyte is commonly abbreviated as M, MB, or Mbyte.

memory Electronic storage area inside the computer, used to temporarily store data or program instructions when the computer is using them. The computer's memory is erased when the power to the computer is turned off.

memory-resident program A program that runs "in the background" while other programs are running, waiting until it is needed.

menu A list of commands or instructions displayed on the screen. Menus organize commands and make a program easier to use.

modem A device that converts your computer's digital data into analog signals that can be sent through a phone line. Another modem on the other end reverses the process, converting the analog back to digital.

mouse A mouse is a device that moves an arrow (a pointer) on the screen. When you move the mouse, the pointer on the screen moves in the same direction. Used instead of the keyboard to select and move items (such as text or graphics), execute commands, and perform other tasks. A mouse gets its name because it connects to your computer through a long "tail" or cord.

MS-DOS (Microsoft Disk Operating System) See *DOS*.

Network See *local area network*.

parameter Extra information that goes along with a command, telling DOS which drives, directories, or files in which to limit its action.

point To position the mouse pointer on-screen so its tip touches an item.

program A set of instructions written in a special "machine language" that the computer understands. Typical programs are word processors, spreadsheets, databases, and games.

program group Similar programs that are grouped together on the Program List to better keep track of them.

program item The name of a program on the Program List.

Program List The area of the DOS Shell screen where commonly used programs wait to be run.

prompt The prompt is a message from DOS letting you know that it is waiting for a command. When you type a command, it will appear next to the prompt on the screen. Typical DOS prompts include **C>** or **C:\DOS>**.

pull-down menu A pull-down menu contains the selections for a main menu command. This type of menu, when activated, is pulled down below the main menu bar, like a window shade can be pulled down from the top of a window frame.

restoring files Backing up your files is a process that copies files onto diskettes in a special compressed format. If those files get damaged somehow, you can restore them through a reverse process that decompresses the backed up files and copies them back.

root directory The top directory on the Directory Tree. Since it doesn't have a directory name, such as DOS or WORD, it is indicated by a plain backslash, as in **C:**.

scroll To move text up/down or right/left on a computer screen.

subdirectories Means the same thing as directories. The prefix sub is used to emphasize the fact that all directories are subordinate to the root directory. Sometimes the word subdirectories is used to describe a directory under another directory.

Switch An optional specification that directs DOS to process the command in a special way.

system diskette A diskette that contains IO.SYS, MSDOS.SYS, and COMMAND.COM, the three files that DOS needs to start itself. Of these, the first two are hidden, so you won't see them when you use DIR to see the disk contents.

text mode A way of displaying a program on-screen so that text and very basic lines are used to simulate pictures. Text mode is a bit drab, but it's speedy, and all monitors can use it.

virus A computer virus is a program that vandalizes your system. The worst viruses destroy data and render your computer helpless. Others simply display strange messages but do no damage. A virus will enter your system through an infected diskette or an infected file that has been downloaded (received through a modem) from another computer.

wild card character A character that stands for any other character. A question mark (?) stands for a single character; an asterisk (*) stands for any number of characters. For example, *.DOC means "a file with any name, of any length, as long as it has an extension of DOC. Here's another: ???.* means "a file with a three-letter name, and any extension of any length.

Windows Often used as a nickname for Microsoft Windows, a graphical interface program.

Index

Symbols

A

B

C

D

E

F

G

H

I-J

N

O

P

Q

R

S

T

U

V

W-Z

A:1 TYPE HIST. WR1.